Reconciliation in the Church

A Theological and Pastoral Essay on the Sacrament of Penance

LÉONCE HAMELIN

Translated by
MATTHEW J. O'CONNELL

THE LITURGICAL PRESS

Collegeville   Minnesota

Library of Congress Cataloging in Publication Data

Hamelin, Léonce.
    Reconciliation in the Church.

    Translation of La réconciliation en Église.
    Bibliography: p.
    1. Penance.   2. Reconciliation.   I. Title.
BX2260.H18713   234'.166   80-29328
ISBN 0-8146-1215-6

NIHIL OBSTAT: Joseph C. Kremer, S.T.L., *Censor Deputatus*
IMPRIMATUR: ✝ George H. Speltz, D.D., Bishop of St. Cloud. October 27, 1980.

RECONCILIATION IN THE CHURCH is the authorized English translation of LA
RÉCONCILIATION EN ÉGLISE by Léonce Hamelin, copyright © 1977 by La Corpora-
tion des Editions Fides, Montreal.

Printed in the United States of America.

ISBN 0-8146-1215-6

Abbreviations

AAS	*Acta Apostolicae Sedis.* Vatican City, 1909 –
CCL	*Corpus Christianorum. Series Latina.* Turnhout, 1953 –
DS	H. Denzinger and A. Schönmetzer, *Enchiridion Symbolorum.* 32nd ed.; Freiburg, 1963.
MGH	*Monumenta Germaniae Historica.* Hannover – Berlin, 1826 –
PL	*Patrologia Latina,* ed. J. P. Migne. Paris, 1844–64.

Contents

Introduction

A brief review of our present situation will surely convince us that reflection on the rite of penance is urgently needed. For this rite is now becoming one of those obsolete items we part from in the same spirit with which we once accepted them: without any special conviction, but also without regret.

Abandonment? Lack of interest? Cultural goods with few buyers? In any event, sinners are increasingly unwilling to put up with the disquietingly gloomy laundry room that the confessional represents. Panic! Can a pastor simply let these indomitable sinners slip away – these people who not only sin unscrupulously but are even proud of themselves? Shall he hunt for ways of restoring the old-time submissive attitude? The stakes are large. The problem is so much out in the open now that it is time to ask public questions of the rite of penance, time to examine, in the light of tradition and modern thought, the value of a sacrament that seems likely soon to vanish from the scene.

As a matter of fact, the question is even more basic: Are Christians shunning the sacraments, or are the sacraments shunning Christians, as it were? The Second Vatican Council gave a clear answer to this question. At the risk of creating drafts and setting people sneezing, the Council called for open windows. The sacraments have felt the stresses and strains of the reform that was then undertaken. New rites have appeared with the purpose of teaching Christians once again to live both really and symbolically as members of the Church. Baptism and marriage have been turned into vital, joyous celebrations.

During this same period, however, the sacrament of reconciliation has been the poor cousin of the family; until now it has received little attention. The Council itself in fact referred only briefly to it: "The rite and formulae of Penance are to be revised so that they more clearly express both the nature and effect of the sacrament."[1] This is perhaps the reason why some people think of the sacrament of penance, the revised rite of which was published in 1973, as resembling one of those stews to which new ingredients are continually being added.

And yet it must be acknowledged that the commission set forth by Vatican II has fallen on receptive ears. Many experiments have been tried by way of response to the Council: communal celebrations have been organized here and there with some success; general absolutions have been given.

But conflicting views are undermining convictions. Many pastors and Christians are asking a blunt question: Is our Church still giving to the world the witness of a community for which conversion is truly a basic value? Others refuse to take part in celebrations of reconciliation on the grounds that they have no right to celebrate the hope of reconciliation as long as serious individual and collective steps have not been taken on behalf of justice, equality and brotherhood. These conflicting views make the very meaning of reconciliation a key issue.

A serious pastoral approach to the problem cannot be satisfied with new recipes; rather it must be guided by meditation on the real import of the evangelical call to repentance. Pastoral experience will doubtless be able, in turn, to direct and enrich such meditation. But, when all is said and done, the essential point is to gain a fuller and deeper understanding of conversion in the Christian perspective, as well as of the ways to forgiveness that Christ has opened for us. A valid answer to the problem may not neglect theological reflection with its two phases or dimensions: careful attention to the data of revelation, and an honest openness to contemporary problems and the legitimate solicitations of the human sciences. It is this kind of reflection that I wish to present in this theological essay on the sacrament of penance. A difficult task, I agree, and one that would discourage even the boldest spirits were it not that others have been working on it for some years now.

As far back as 1950, on the occasion of the Congress of Spirituality held in Rome, pastors were beginning to be uneasy at the decreasing frequency with which people were going to confession. Questionnaires multiplied, but they only made the extent of the crisis clearer. Criticism of the penitential rite was severe, even extreme. Nor was the discontent with sacramental penance to be explained solely by a lessening of faith. It was due also, and perhaps above all, to the rejection of a meaningless sacramental ritual. Against this background we can understand the pressures within the Church that led the Council Fathers to call for a far-reaching reform of the penitential rite. After ten years of study and research the International Committee on the Liturgy presented a new rite of penance, and the Congregation for Divine Worship approved it on December 2, 1973.

The introduction of the new rite was soon followed by theological commentaries and pastoral reflections. In the United States, for example, the Catholic Theological Society of America published in 1975 the report of a committee established three years earlier "to explore the renewal of the sacrament of penance in the life of the Church."[2] Among the practical considerations made by this committee were invitations to biblical scholars and to moral, systematic, and pastoral theologians to study and reevaluate such areas as the meaning of redemption, the relationship of grace and sin, the possibility of sacramental absolution without individual confession of sins, and the conversion of the mentality of the faithful from the attitude that asks, "Is this a sin?" to the spirit that ponders, "How can I love more?"[3]

Again in 1975 the United States' Bishops' Committee on the Liturgy published a study text of the new rite of penance.[4] In addition to a general treatment of sin, penance, and reconciliation, this booklet offered a pastoral commentary on the introduction to the new rite along with a thorough discussion of the three forms of sacramental reconciliation.

In my own country, the Canadian Theological Society was early consulted by the Canadian episcopate. It advised the bishops to appoint a commission that would devote careful study to the matter. Among other recommendations the commission proposed that a pastoral directory for penance be composed. A draft of such a directory was presented to the bishops in March, 1974. There was no follow-up, however, on the report; understandably enough, the episcopal conference could take no steps in matters liturgical without the all but unanimous agreement of its members. As a result, therefore, the Christian people received the impression that nothing was being done. Meanwhile, many of them were cherishing the illusory hope that along with the confessional the sacrament of penance itself would disappear, like other outmoded practices of the Church.

Pastoral practice, for its part, has followed a normal pattern of development. Pastors have made extensive use of the communal rite of penance, especially before Christmas and Easter. This rite would seem to pave the way for general absolution, which the Church authorized in June, 1972.[5] These pastoral practices have received serious and thorough evaluation.

The present study of the sacrament of penance will take into account all this work that has already been done. It has also profited by the many meetings of priests that I have been able to attend. Its chief point of reference, however, is the new *Rite of Penance* (1973).[6] I shall analyze its theological and pastoral implications; this is to say that I shall try to set up a critical framework for a better understanding of the experience of this sacrament, with a view to meaningful pastoral action.

Clearly enough, it is not my task to find surefire ways of bringing Christians back to confession. My aim is rather to elucidate, with as little distortion as possible, the intention of Jesus that gives meaning to the repentance and reconciliation of sinners.

Taking as my starting point the idea that the penitential rite should be flexible enough to respond to the basic aspirations of the faithful, I shall first of all establish the problematic within which I intend to work. The analysis of the data of Christian experience, both biblical and ecclesial, will bring out the important values of reconciliation in the Church. It will then be possible to understand, in faith, the process of conversion and of its expression in the Christian community. From this the pastoral implications should emerge clearly enough to allow, finally, a judicious application of the penitential rite.[7]

1

Why a Sacrament of Reconciliation?

1

In Search of a Problematic

A sacrament losing its vigor

The decreasing frequency with which people receive the sacrament of penance is a readily observable fact. It involves not only those who are negligent about the practice of their faith or who have no great love of the Church, but also fervent Christians, religious and priests. Moreover, this state of affairs has been spreading throughout all Catholic countries for about twenty-five years now.

The extensive data compiled in various places[1] and the conclusions drawn from them enable us to evaluate with greater precision and accuracy what is going on at present in pastoral practice with regard to the sacrament of penance.

One way of summing up our present situation would be in the lapidary sentence: "Christians do not have faith any more." If we take this as our starting point, it will not surprise us that there is a falling off in religious practice and that the sacrament of penance is affected by this general collapse.

This approach has something to say for it but it is too sweeping, and, if we go no further, it is likely to focus our attention on too narrow a problem. This is a point I need not insist on. We must start with a more comprehensive view of the problem.

Some of the many causes

What has happened to turn confession, formerly so popular, into something taboo? After an inquiry into the practice of this sacrament, the Canadian Theological Society wrote as follows in its preliminary report to the bishops:

7

Speaking generally, we may say that too few of the faithful seem to have had a positive experience of the sacrament of penance; even the most committed Christians do not always manage to grasp the significance of this action in the Christian life as a whole. Speaking more particularly, we can point to many reasons why the present attitude to penance has developed. Here, briefly, are some of them:

— a defective understanding of God and sin;

— a shift in the perception of moral values, for example in the area of sexuality;

— an unevangelical idea of conversion as a restoration of harmony with the law or with oneself and one's moral ideal, instead of an encounter with the Father;

— an insensitivity to the ecclesial dimension of salvation;

— a rejection of the (often rigid) categories of mortal and venial sin;

— a rejection of the idea that a person can so readily lose and regain the friendship of God;

— the feeling that in the celebration of the sacrament the accusation is disproportionately emphasized to the detriment of other values: evangelization, conversion, and reparation.[2]

Such a detailed list is likely to be rather complete. Even so, it does not suffice as the basis for a valid statement of the problem. It does not provide a reliable reading grill by which to direct our reflections, if for no other reason than that it is too scattered.

When I question those who still go to confession, I receive answers nearly identical with those I have received from young people in secondary school. Without claiming a complete list, I offer some of the statements made in answer to the question: "Why do you go to confession?"

"I feel consolation after confession."

"If I do not confess, I feel remorse."

"Confession sets me free."

"God is a friend whom I meet in confession."

"It is a meeting with God."

"Confession gives me an opportunity to think, and restores my union with God."

"I receive forgiveness."

"I am reunited to God after breaking with him."

"The sacrament removes my sins."

"God strengthens us and helps us to live better lives."
"Purification and a better life thereafter."
"A renewal."
"This sacrament helps us in our lives."

It is not for me to decide whether the practice of sacramental penance by those who thus replied to the question resulted from conviction or was simply an echo of what they had once been taught. In any case, a striking fact emerges: the sacrament is understood in various ways, as a *liberation,* an *encounter,* a *forgiveness,* a *spiritual renewal.*[3]

I have repeated here only such answers as were expressed in the language of faith, and have deliberately omitted those that were too exclusively sociological in character, such as the desire to please someone, or the insistence of parents (this still occurs), or the desire to avoid complications, or the inquisitorial gaze of bystanders (at communal celebrations), and so on.[4]

But even when located within a context of faith, the answers I have cited do not manifest a very clear understanding of the sacrament of penance and, in many instances, would not justify the institution of a special sacrament for the sake of the purposes indicated. All the sacraments, after all, are encounters with the Lord, as is prayer; the Eucharist can be a source of spiritual renewal; baptism, the anointing of the sick, and the Eucharist are also means of obtaining forgiveness. In what manner, then, does penance bring forgiveness and liberation? The desire for conversion plays little part in the answers given, despite the ringing call of the scriptures to conversion and to the repentance that wins the forgiveness of our sins: "Repent, therefore, and turn again, that your sins may be blotted out" (Acts 3:19).

Ignorance of the true meaning of the sacrament has led many Christians — sometimes their whole life long — to regard the penitential rite as a bit of magical sham. The absolution of the priest is thought to get rid of sin the way a cleaning agent removes a spot from a garment. Just perform the action correctly, and "the trick is done"!

Juridical formalism does exist — much too much of it, unfortunately. It is based on a very narrow understanding of auricular confession. To improve the situation, all that was needed was to modify our sacramental rite. That is what some have tried to do. But then they should not have reintroduced the juridical machinery into the new rite that was adopted to cure the original disease! After long sessions in the confessional, many confessors began to doubt the value of those interminable hours, especially at Christmas and Easter. But many of them now feel the same doubt regarding the absolutions they distribute in response to the mechanical accusations that the recent communal rite has made customary!

Let us not be too quick to blame the pious faithful. They were subjected to a skeletal ritual. The whole business took place in a smelly box that admitted neither light nor air nor any breath of humanity that might freshen the atmosphere of this meeting. It was a meeting of two human beings who were unable to carry on a dialogue, for one of them thought of himself as "Jesus Christ," while the other thought of himself or herself as a potential "demon."

Only with difficulty could this kind of formalism touch the heart of the penitent and make possible the beginnings of a conversion. Most penitents went away unaffected.

And yet we must not generalize too much. I know of happy exceptions, and many confessors have nostalgic memories of penitents who left the confessional in tears. They will complain now that "general absolution will never have that kind of effect!" That a good confession had a liberating effect is beyond doubt; it is less certain that confessions always had such an effect. Besides, if treatment of a psychological kind is what is wanted, recourse should be had to a psychiatrist or psychologist rather than a priest – and that is precisely the choice many of our contemporaries have made! If a pastor is also an able psychologist, well and good, but that is certainly not his primary role.

The loss of the sense of sin

This first set of observations will have shown us that many Christians have lost the meaning of the sacrament of penance. Let me turn now to a complementary point. How often we hear the commonplace: "There is no longer such a thing as 'sin'; confession has lost its point. What is the Church waiting for? Why doesn't she get rid of this useless, outmoded contrivance?" If people think of penance solely as a means of washing sin away, it is quite natural to think of the machinery as useless once there is no longer anything to wash away.

Some people will believe themselves justified in thinking that sin has disappeared, because the old lists of sins have disappeared. Actions formerly regarded as sinful are today regarded as indifferent or even beneficial. Brother Untel, of happy memory, remarked once that some Christians – "old-timers," admittedly – found themselves at a loss when the Church eliminated some big sins which nicely filled out their annual list of accusations (fasting, abstinence, holydays of obligation). A witty observation? Of course, but I think it also pinpointed an important *situation*.

When certain obligations such as fasting and abstinence were removed, too many Christians failed to realize that the Church was telling them to cultivate a personal sense of duty with regard to real and abiding values. When she removed from the books laws established in a bygone era, she had no intention of abolishing with them such traditional and evangelical values as penance. On the contrary, her desire was to revitalize them by bringing them before the Christian conscience, but in a different way. The unfortunate thing is that those responsible for evangelization did not devote a comparable care to the formation of conscience among the Christian people. Without such updated instruction and formation, people were given an opportunity to cultivate the notion that sin had disappeared. It became very difficult to remedy the new situation effectively.

Meanwhile, cocktail-party chitchat had had time to produce its effects. This was the weakness of our old lists of sins: the nature of sin itself was blurred and the distinction between mortal and venial sin became confused. As a result, people were no longer clear on what they ought to be confessing; from this it was a short step to deciding not to confess at all.

However, we should not think of our contemporaries as blinder than they really are. Like people of other times, they are, if anything, only too ready to criticize and find fault with others for deceiving themselves and believing that evil no longer exists. But the points of view have changed.

Christian life as a comprehensive project

The typically modern person thinks of life less as a discontinuous succession of moments or distinct actions that cannot be considered in isolation. Moderns look at life rather as a totality that is undergirded by a project, a basic choice of good or evil. A morality of dispositions or attitudes tends to replace a morality of acts; "sin" covers more than sins.

People today take as the point of reference for conscience a moral project that is coextensive with life in its entirety (here and now, and through time). There is no more use for a life made up of detachable segments, each of which can be evaluated as a separate entity. Value attaches rather to the meaning that life has as a whole. Sin, consequently, consists first and foremost in deviating from one's project, in changing direction, in retrogressing morally. It is therefore possible to evaluate the presence of sin only at intervals and from a distance. Correlatively, it is difficult to pass judgment on a particular moment of life, as is done when sin is conceived as a failure to obey the moral law in an isolated action.

Under the influence, again, of their times, modern Christians have difficulty in conceiving of themselves as isolated individuals; they exist only in a network of relations. In general, they are interested primarily in "horizontal" relations: relations with nature and with their fellow human beings. They are concerned to protect the environment and build the world. Quite naturally, therefore, they tend to locate evil at the points where this task is notably compromised. This is the kind of sin that we can see; we can detect its consequences; we can put our finger on it.

This sort of horizontalism evidently has both advantages and drawbacks. In one direction, it has refined the moral conscience by making it more attentive and sensitive to wrongs done to the neighbor. But there is another side to the coin: The fact that sin disturbs our relationship with God is rather left in the background. It must be admitted, of course, that the theologians have always had trouble seeing just how God can be offended. Everyone knows the classical objection: How can a human action affect the godhead? Today it is the very reality of such an offense that is challenged and the existential experience of it that is imperiled. The experience of seeing oneself as a sinner before God and in relation to him is becoming increasingly rare and may even be regarded as an alienating illusion.

What was said above about the sense of sin can now be reformulated. The sense of sin, which in the past focused on a list of sins, tends to express itself in our contemporaries in the acknowledgment that they are in a sinful state to the extent that they are associated with and participate in human actions that are too complex to be broken down into simple actions and then codified. A second characteristic of the contemporary conscience is the tendency to conceive its projects no longer in terms primarily of the individual but rather as collective duties. People are certainly ready to acknowledge their personal responsibility, but they also have a much keener awareness than in the past of the collective dimension of sin, the importance of co-responsibility, and the interdependence of human beings in formulating the great projects that fill a lifetime. It is not surprising that this new awareness of community seeks expression in actions that will be a due and adequate translation of it.

The penitential rite: A means of realizing one's sins?

These observations suggest a question: Should not one purpose of the penitential rite be to provide an opportunity for persons to become aware of their sins as realities having both a social and a personal dimension? Perhaps we have looked at the sacrament too exclusively as providing a mechanical forgiveness of sins.[5]

We may put the question more explicitly: What is the basic meaning to be given to the sacrament of penance so that the Church will be part of it; so that sinners will not isolate themselves in a barren sense of guilt; and so that the sacrament will rather send them back renewed to their human and Christian responsibilities in the world and in history? Can penance not bring to full consciousness the new meaning that Jesus Christ has given to human life? Can it not stimulate human beings to live the new life that is really theirs? It has all it needs to accomplish this task in a sacramental manner, that is, in a direct encounter with a minister of the Church, with the "other" that is the ecclesial community, thus making it obvious that purification, forgiveness, and liberation do not come from the minister nor from the community but from Another, the Second Adam, and, above all, from a God who loves them.

It is an undeniable fact that today's Christians do not understand the meaning of the sacrament of penance. On the other hand, they do experience within themselves a profound desire for liberation and for reconciliation with their neighbors, with themselves, and (why not just as much?) with God. They need to be told that they are saved in Jesus Christ.

This brings us to consider sacramental penance as an event that is celebrated in the Church and that gives Christians an opportunity to express their faith in the salvation Jesus has accomplished, to acknowledge their failure in regard to the salvation Christ proclaims, to ask the Lord for true communion with the members of the community, and to receive from the Church the sign of God's forgiveness.[6]

Let us see now whether the problematic as I have stated it can stand up to a confrontation with the biblical and ecclesial tradition. In other words, whether it fits in with the thinking of Jesus.

2

The Church as Place of Reconciliation

Why is it that we have reconciliation in the Church? In the first chapter I have tried to answer this question by appealing to the evidence of contemporary Christian experience. Let us look now at what the biblical tradition has to say on the subject.

I shall take as my point of departure the relevant terms most frequently used in the scriptures. In this way we shall see what is implied in the call to conversion that meets us on every page of the Bible. In the process we shall find that this call to conversion is also a summons to "confession." But does "confession" require a particular rite? This we shall attempt to determine before analyzing all the basic implications of this act of confession.[1]

1. Call to conversion

Conversion and repentance play an important role in biblical revelation. However, the terms used to express these ideas only gradually acquired their full meaning, according as the notion of sin underwent development. The term most frequently used expresses the idea of changing one's course, turning back, tracing one's steps. In a religious context, it means that a person turns away from evil and turns back to God. In this we have the essence of conversion that implies a change of behavior, a new direction for the whole of one's activity.

A distinction is made between the interior aspect of repentance and the external actions that it necessitates. Thus the Greek Bible links the verbs *epistrephein,* referring to a change of conduct, and *metanoein,* referring to the interior turning.

15

Especially in the prophets we find a progressive purification of the idea of conversion. Hosea attacks ritual used as magic and calls for "steadfast love and not sacrifice, the knowledge of God, rather than burnt offerings" (6:6). Amos criticizes external forms that do not bring out with sufficient clarity the relation that should exist between God and a sinner: "Take away from me the noise of your songs; to the melody of your harps I will not listen. But let justice roll down like waters, and righteousness like an everflowing stream" (5:23-24).

In other words, the prophets wax angry at penitential practices that have become lifeless and meaningless. In so doing, they make clear to us the dimension of depth that is proper to conversion. On the other hand, as von Rad rightly points out, the purpose of prophetic criticism is not a one-sided spiritualization of cultic concepts, but rather the forging of a link between the external gestures and the human heart.[2] The essential point in their eyes is not that sinners should simply be present in body among the multitude of penitents, but rather that their inner selves should be focused on the God who challenges individuals in their entirety and without qualification. In addition, the most important matter is not isolated sins that are to be expiated; the real issue is the entire sinful self that seeks to avoid the punishments due its sins and thus to create a new relationship between Yahweh and the repentant sinner.

In these perspectives, sin comes to be seen increasingly as something expressive of the person; it shows its presence in individual, visible actions. Repentance consists in turning completely to Yahweh with unconditional trust, for God's help is utterly indispensable. The person must turn away from what is not God. Such a turning is admittedly difficult, but it is not impossible, since conversion is to be seen as first and foremost an action of God.

This particular aspect of conversion calls for special attention. On the one hand, conversion requires that sinners make an effort to abandon their evil ways. Thus both Jeremiah and Ezekiel exhort sinners to convert and reach true life: "Thus says the Lord: Stand in the court of the Lord's house, and speak to all the cities of Judah which come to worship in the house of the Lord all the words that I command you to speak to them; do not hold back a word. It may be they will listen, and every one turn from his evil way, that I may repent of the evil which I intend to do to them because of their evil doings" (Jer 26:2-3; see 36:3). "Have I any pleasure in the death of the wicked, says the Lord God, and not rather that he should turn from his way and live?" (Ezek 18:23; see 3:18). Ezekiel, especially, emphasizes the need of turning from evil: "But if you warn the wicked, and he does not turn from his wickedness, or from his wicked way, he shall die in his iniquity; but you will have saved your life" (3:19; see 18:21, 23, 27).

On the other hand, these same prophets accept it as a principle that conversion depends on an action of God: "But this is the covenant which I will make with the house of Israel after those days, says the Lord: I will put my law within them, and I will write it upon their hearts; and I will be their God, and they shall be my people. And no longer shall each man teach his neighbor and each his brother, saying, 'Know the Lord,' for they shall all know me, from the least to the greatest, says the Lord; for I will forgive their iniquity, and I will remember their sin no more" (Jer 31:33-34; see 13:23). "A new heart I will give you, and a new spirit I will put within you; and I will take out of your flesh the heart of stone and give you a heart of flesh. And I will put my spirit within you, and cause you to walk in my statutes and be careful to observe my ordinances" (Ezek 36:26-27; see 11:19).

Conversion is thus regarded as an action of God toward the person, but also as an action of the individual. In order to bring out the full impact of these texts, I shall put a few of them in parallel columns:

Role of the person	**Role of God**
Invitation to conversion:	Jer 31:18: "Bring me back that I may
Jer 36:3: (Be converted) "so that everyone may turn from his evil way, and that I may forgive their iniquity and their sin."	be restored, for thou art the Lord my God."
	Ezek 36:26-31: "a new heart . . . a new spirit. . . ."
Conditions for conversion:	
acknowledge your guilt (Jer 3:13)	
change your ways (4:1, 4)	
and do not simply weep (3:21-25)	

The preaching of John the Baptist and of Jesus follow in the line of the prophets. It is more categorical, of course, in John than in the prophets because God's action toward his people is imminent. The call to conversion is addressed henceforth not only to sinners — "Tax collectors also came to be baptized, and said to [John], 'Teacher, what shall we do?' And he said to them, 'Collect no more than is appointed you' (Lk 3:12-13) — or to pagans — "Soldiers also asked [John], 'And we, what shall we do?'" (Lk 3:14) — but even to the devout who think they have no need of conversion — "But when [Jesus] saw many of the Pharisees and Sadducees coming for baptism, he said to them, 'You brood of vipers! Who warned you to flee from the wrath to come? Bear fruit that befits repentance, and do not presume to say to yourselves, "We have Abraham as our father"; for I tell you, God is able to raise up children to Abraham. Even now the axe is laid to the root of the trees; every tree therefore that does not bear good fruit is cut down and thrown into the fire'" (Mt 3:7-10). Conversion must be proved by conduct in the whole of life — "Bear fruit that befits repentance" (Mt 3:8; see Lk 3:10-14). To this extent, conversion is an action of the individual. But since John the Baptist connects his preaching with a baptism of repentance (Mk 1:4), conversion becomes an eschatological gift that the person must receive from God.

Jesus, for his part, asserts that salvation is already present in the kingdom that is now becoming a reality; the call to conversion refers to the present moment. He offers no way of return apart from himself; he is the sole way of salvation. Christ has come "to call . . . sinners to repentance" (Lk 5:32). This is an essential part of the good news of the kingdom.

But while Jesus calls for conversion, he makes no reference to any penitential liturgies. He even distrusts signs that are too obtrusive — "And when you fast, do not look dismal, like the hypocrites . . ." (Mt 6:16-18). The important thing is that the heart should turn and become like that of a little child (Mt 18:3). The next step is an ongoing effort to "seek first his kingdom and his righteousness" (Mt 6:33), that is, an ordering of one's life according to the new Law, in which the act of conversion is pictured in eloquent parables. The effort at conversion implies a desire for moral change, but it finds expression above all in a humble appeal, an act of trust: "God, be merciful to me a sinner!" (Lk 18:13).

2. Conversion and confession

In the biblical tradition conversion takes the form of a *profession of faith*. This profession developed gradually in connection with a set of ritual practices. The confession of sins, though not yet expressly linked to the sacrament of penance, is always mentioned in a context of penitential rites. The admission of one's situation as sinner is seen as an essential gesture in every penitential rite and as a profoundly meaningful action.

The New Testament speaks of confession as a current practice. The baptismal rite used by John includes a personal confession of sins by the baptized: "They were baptized by him in the Jordan, confessing their sins" (Mk 1:5; Mt 3:6). The converts at Ephesus prove the genuineness of their repentance by confessing their magical practices (Acts 19:18). St. James urges Christians to confess their sins to one another (Jas 5:16), while St. John speaks of the external confession of sins, and not just a general acknowledgment of one's sinful state, as being a condition for obtaining God's forgiveness (1 Jn 1:9).

The New Testament references to the need of an external confession of sins may seem rather sparse, but in fact they only repeat a norm that had long been generally accepted in Israel. It was an unchallenged truth that the confession of sins was necessary if forgiveness was to be obtained: "He who conceals his transgressions will not prosper, but he who confesses and forsakes them will obtain mercy" (Prov 28:13). The equivalent of this stylized assertion of the wisdom writers is to be found in the priestly tradition — "When a man is guilty in any of these [transgressions], he shall confess the sin he has committed, and he shall bring his guilt offering to the Lord for the sin which he has committed, a female from the flock, a lamb or a goat, for a sin offering; and the priest shall make atonement for him for his sin" (Lev 5:5-6) — and especially in the Psalms, Israel's prayerbook — for example, "I acknowledged my sin to thee, and I did not hide my iniquity; I said, 'I will confess my transgressions to the Lord'; then thou didst forgive the guilt of my sin" (Ps 32:5; see Ps

38:4-6, 18; 41:4; 51:3-5). Toward the end of the Old Testament national disasters lead to a public confession of all the sins of the people, who are represented by one of their number (Dan 3:28-29; 9:4-19; Jdt 9:1-14; Bar 1:15–2:10; Tob 3:1-6, 11-15). In addition to these exceptional circumstances, the annual feast of atonement (see Lev 16) has for its purpose to obtain God's pardon for all of Israel by means of a public confession and a sacrifice.

The need of confession continues to be asserted during the intertestamental period (Psalms of Solomon 9:6; 3 Mac 2:2-20; 6:2-15), especially at Qumran, where the annual feast of covenant renewal includes a general confession of sins.[3] The rabbinical schools also stress the obligation of confessing one's sins: it is possible to think of one who confesses as "being in the same situation as a robber before his judge. As long as the robber protests his innocence he is not condemned, but when he admits his guilt he is condemned. Yet it is not so with God: as long as the human being refuses to confess, he or she is condemned; but as soon as confession is made, the words of liberation follow."[4]

In all the passages cited above there is never a question of a purely interior confession addressed directly to God. This type of avowal, in the form of a purely interior admission, would be intelligible in the Greek world but would be utterly inconceivable to a Semite. For the Semite, a person is so much a unit that a repentance that does not change the whole person is simply not genuine. What to a Greek would be a mere bodily expression and quite secondary or even marginal by comparison with the spiritual reality of repentance becomes for the Semite a manifestation that is inseparable from the interior will to conversion. The word (almost a technical term) used to express the confession of sins is *exhomologesis,*[5] and the prefix *ex* implies that the confession is something public.

The point that emerges most strikingly from the biblical texts that deal with the confession of sins is the close and constant connection between avowal and gratitude to God, between the human confession of the self as sinful and the confession of God as redeemer.

The Septuagint and the New Testament use the two verbs *homologein* and *exhomologein* to mean at times "to confess" God, at times "to confess" one's sins to God, but the first of the two meanings predominates (e.g., in the New Testament seventeen out of twenty-two occurrences). The two meanings are so readily accepted that Paul can cite Is 45:23 — "As I live, says the Lord, every knee shall bow to me, and every tongue shall confess to God" — as referring to the eschatological confession of sins that every individual must make before the throne of God (Rom 14:11), and yet implicitly cite the same text in Phil 2:10-11 to express thanksgiving to God: ". . . at the name of Jesus every knee should bow, . . . and every tongue confess that Jesus Christ is Lord to the glory of God the Father."

In the public worship of ancient Israel the confession of human guilt was already associated with thanksgiving to God. We see this association in the liturgies of sacrifice for sin and in hymns of thanksgiving (Ps 22; 30; 34; 40; 116; Hannah's prayer in 1 Sam 2:1-10; King Hezekiah's plea and praise in Is 38:9-20; and Raguel's blessing in Tob 8:15-17). God is praised because he delivers someone from a serious danger. Thus in Job 33:19-26, Elihu shows how sickness had brought a man to the point of death, but then God took pity on him and healed him. Thereupon the one who had recovered comes before the people and confesses: "I sinned, and perverted what was right, and it was not requited to me. He has redeemed my soul from going down into the Pit, and my life shall see the light" (vv. 27–28).

The reason why the Old and New Testaments regularly associate the confession of sins with thanksgiving is that the entire biblical tradition sees the association as reflecting a profound truth. In the Bible praise almost always has the merciful action of God in history as its theme. But if God's action is to affect persons as conscious beings, then they must acknowledge their need and admit their poverty before God. Now, in fact, all the sufferings and degradations of human beings have their origin in sin. They must therefore confess their sin and guilt if they are to be able to receive the regenerating action of God. This help from God is so certain that the verb for the confession of sins also means a confession of the mercy of God, who stoops to those who humble themselves before him.

3. Confession and penitential rite

Is it possible to take a further step in our reading of the Bible and uncover other indications regarding a penitential rite? It is indeed! For repentance has another important dimension: its aspect as reconciliation.

In the Old Testament sin is not primarily a matter of one's private relation to God. This is true because the ordinances and commandments of Yahweh, which sin violates, are not directives addressed to the person as an isolated entity. Taken as a whole, the commands are an expression of the covenant between God and his people; they become *Torah* (Law) only to the extent that law *embodies* and *guarantees* the covenant. The covenant is violated by the complaints and rejections of the people as a body, but it is not less violated when a single individual rebels against the Law and departs from it. In fact, this kind of behavior affects the relation of Israel itself with the God of the covenant.

When seen in this perspective, the Israelite practice of banishment belongs to the theological order, whatever be the other factors that concretely determine the existence of the phenomenon. The wicked person must be removed from the midst of Israel (Deut 13:6ff.), because the nation is a holy people and must remain such: "So you shall purge the evil from the midst of you" (Deut 13:5).

We find evidence of the same practice in the Qumran texts, and specifically in the Rule's regulations regarding the isolation of members.[6] Major faults against the law of the brotherhood, against the authority of the "watchman" or the council, and against fraternal charity were punished by a fairly lengthy exclusion (up to two years) or even by dismissal; if the punishment was exclusion, the repentant sinner could be received back.

Despite qualitative differences at various stages, the saving action of God toward the human race is marked by an evident continuity. Understandably, then, in her manner of judging sin in her midst and of dealing with sinners (warning, punishing, interceding), the Church of Jesus retains the attitudes and practices that had developed in the world from which she sprang.

When people touched by grace decide to enter the Church of Jesus (first conversion), when as believers they accept his message as authoritative, and when through baptism they have been received into the Church, then they share in the holiness of the Church, and this in a way of which Old Testament revelation gave no inkling. When people become Christians, they are essentially liberated from sin, as the teaching of the Pauline epistles makes clear.

And yet men and women are many-sided and subject to the testing of time. It is to be expected, therefore, that they will not always go unscathed. The human situation is reflected in the hortatory parts of the Pauline letters and in the very real danger pointed out in the same letters that Christians may fall back to a former state, live in accordance with the present world, the *sarx* ("flesh"), and thus become sinners. In addition, the entire New Testament, including the gospels, refers to sins that Christians – the disciples and even the Apostles – do in fact commit.

The New Testament sees the Church as the body or bride of Christ, as the temple or house of God, and as the one that introduces order into nature. In consequence, every sin committed in the Church is necessarily an *offense,* an *insult* against God who has cleansed the community by means of his Son's blood. We must add that by its very nature the Church is so close-knit a community that a sin of a member against God alone, or a sin that remains seemingly interior, in fact offends the Church herself.

Therefore we must not think of the penitential practice of the early Church as resulting from a kind of extrinsic, arbitrary decree of God. Neither must we think of it as representing the survival of frozen traditions and borrowings from Israel. No, the very theology of the Church in the New Testament is at stake here.

The adequate response of the Church to the sins of her members is to separate the sinners from herself, and to do it in such a way that the separation is visible to all. By this kind of evident exclusion the Church enables everyone to understand what sinners have done to themselves. This action of separating sinners is thus important for their eternal salvation. In the penitential practice of the New Testament there is no question of a purification of the Church that would be purely external and disciplinary.

At the same time, it would be contrary to the message of Jesus and the ethos of his preaching if this official sentence of exile should be definitive. The Church must remain open to repentant sinners and to the entire human race so as to grant forgiveness to all who are converted.

It is, then, with a full awareness of her mission that the Church excludes sinners after exhorting, warning, and reprimanding them. She has neither the power nor the mission to send them off to their definitive damnation. Even when thus separated from the community of God, sinners profit by the Church's prayers for their correction and amendment, and this fact has an influence on their eternal destiny that will come to light on the Day of the Lord. In the New Testament no penitential procedure is without the perspective of forgiveness for those who have cut themselves off, provided they repent. The concluding advice in 2 Thess is especially pertinent: "If any one refuses to obey what we say in this letter, note that man, and have nothing to do with him, that he may be ashamed. Do not look on him as an enemy, but warn him as a brother" (3:14-15; see 1 Cor 5:1ff.; 2 Thess 3:6; 1 Tim 1:20).

Nevertheless, given several factors — the state of unbroken expectation in which the early Church lived, the psychological attitude of all new converts, and, finally, the fact that the young Church was not accustomed to serious sin in her midst — we should be prepared not to find in scripture any more explicit mention of penitential practice. Nevertheless, 2 Cor 2:5-11 certainly gives a case of reconciliation with the Church: "But if any one has caused pain, he has caused it not to me, but in some measure — not to put it too severely — to you all. For such a one this punishment by the majority is enough; so you should rather turn to forgive and comfort him, or he may be overwhelmed by excessive sorrow. . . ." And when Paul urges Timothy not to impose hands hastily (1 Tim 5:22) and not to participate in another person's sins, he can be understood as speaking of forgiveness.

At the very least, the following words to the Corinthians certainly express the conviction that the Church is the normal locus of reconciliation: "Therefore, if any one is in Christ, he is a new creation; the old has passed away, behold, the new has come. All this is from God, who through Christ reconciled us to himself and gave us the ministry of reconciliation; that is, God was in Christ reconciling the world to himself, not counting their trespasses against them, and entrusting to us the message of reconciliation. So we are ambassadors for Christ, God making his appeal through us. We beseech you on behalf of Christ, be reconciled to God" (2 Cor 5:17-20).

4. The implications of the penitential rite

If we analyze, in the perspectives here set forth, the three New Testament texts to which Christian tradition most often appeals (Mt 18:15-22; Jn 20:19-23; Jas 5:16-20), we will find the dimensions of the penitential rite becoming clearer. There is no doubt that the texts refer to dealings with individuals; at the same time, however, the communal dimension is so clearly indicated that we are surprised not to see later tradition retaining a better grasp of it.

I shall not offer a complete exegesis of these texts,[7] but shall concentrate on two particular points: the common responsibility of all Christians in the act of conversion, and the great importance of community prayer for the sinner.

Matthew 18:15-22

Let us look first at the context in which this passage is found. The main theme is a call to conversion: "Truly, I say to you, unless you turn . . . you will never enter the kingdom of heaven" (18:3). This conversion must be made unpretentiously, after the manner of a child (vv. 4-5), but it must be sincere and effective, to the point of avoiding all scandal, even that which consists in leading the weak astray (vv. 6-10). At this point is inserted the parable of the lost sheep (vv. 12-14) which shows the part a pastor plays in the conversion of a sinner. In verse 15 the entire Christian community is seen aiding in the conversion of the brothers and sisters.

When Christians sin, it is the duty of the whole Church to respond. "Seek them out," the text tells us, not in order to humiliate them, but in a spirit of love. Speak to them face to face (we might say today), with a consciousness of your personal responsibility as a member of the Church. The parable of the lost sheep emphasized the duty of pastors; now the focus is on the individual responsibility of Christians. "If one member suffers, all suffer together" (1 Cor

12:26). In a number of other texts we find this same emphasis on watchfulness over one another. For example, "Brethren, if a man is overtaken in any trespass, you who are spiritual should restore him in a spirit of gentleness. Look to yourself, lest you too be tempted" (Gal 6:1; see Jas 5:19-20; 1 Cor 12:21). Finally, we may note the emphasis on the patience Christians must have in dealing with recalcitrant sinners: far from giving up after the first rejection, we should make further efforts to convince the sinner, but always in a prudent and loving way.

Analysis shows that the text is not a set of rules but an instruction on the proper application of community discipline; this suggests, of course, that such a discipline existed. Jesus and the evangelists after him do not establish rules; the passage presupposes that such rules exist and are valid but that the important thing is to apply them prudently and without forgetting the need of first trying a private exhortation.[8] Since God's will is that no one should be lost, the community must avoid "excommunicating" a sinful brother or sister. The emphasis is on the individual character of the reprimand. The point here is not to assemble the entire community for the purpose of making the person's sin known, but rather to exhort the sinner to repent as a member of a community he or she is on the point of abandoning (see 1 Cor 9:19-22).

The next step is to "quarantine" the sinner, a step expressed in the words: "Let him be to you as a Gentile or a tax collector." Gentile and tax collector symbolize all who are alien to the Church, people with whom one has nothing in common. Clearly, the reference is not to a physical act of expulsion, but rather to open recognition of a fact in the presence of the community. Sinners in fact exclude themselves from the community of the faithful.

The next verses are more difficult. "Truly, I say to you . . .": the connection with what precedes is here established rather artificially. Furthermore, to whom does the "you" refer? To the Apostles, that is, a group with special prerogatives? To the disciples, that is, all Christians taken individually? To the Church, that is, the entire community of Christians that will henceforth act by mandate? All three interpretations have been defended.

One interpretation identifies the "you" with the Apostles as possessors and representatives of hierarchic ecclesiastical authority. This is the interpretation held by the Council of Trent and repeated in the new Rite of Penance.[9] Further on, I shall come back to the theological arguments which led the Church to adopt this interpretation. From the exegetical viewpoint, the interpretation is difficult to defend.

It is quite certain that Matthew has placed the passage in a context in which it was not originally found. With this as their starting point, some exegetes have supposed that the passage had been taken from a context in which it was addressed to a limited group, namely, the Apostles. The deduction is plausible, but on the other hand Matthew deliberately places it in a discourse addressed to the "disciples," and he never limits the term "disciples" to the Apostles alone; the word refers rather to the collection of churches, that is, to all those who believe in Christ and who are addressed as brothers and sisters.

The passage may also be connected with the preceding parable. In the parable of the lost sheep, the community certainly has someone whose duty it is to bring the sinner back, namely the "good shepherd," the person in authority over the community. But this special responsibility of his does not mean that each member of the community does not also have a responsibility.

It would be clearly wrong to believe that all Christians together and each individually have the power to bind and loose, "power" being taken in a democratic sense. This individualistic interpretation has been defended in the Anglican tradition; the Council of Trent rightly rejects it,[10] though without giving any positive interpretation in its place. The context suggests that the "you" is all the "disciples" or the local community. This "communal you" occurs often in the New Testament, especially in the letters. We may compare "He who hears you, hears me," where there is a similar reference to conversion within the community.

This interpretation in no way diminishes the need Christians have of forgiving one another's sins (recall Jas 5:16: "Confess your sins to one another"); in fact, our present text makes this point explicitly a little further on when Peter asks how often he must forgive another — seven times? No, rather seventy times seven (vv. 21-22). The passage is thus telling us that the two gestures of reconciliation, the individual and the communal, are complementary, even while attributing to the communal a special importance that will lead the Church to see in it a sacramental action.

This passage from Matthew contains two further emphases that have perhaps not been given the attention they deserve. One is the importance of prayer, the other is the limitless nature of forgiveness. These emphases further accentuate the communal dimension of the penitential rite.[11]

"If two of you agree on earth about anything they ask . . ." (vv. 19-20). These two verses are quite frequently taken to be a general statement of Jesus about prayer, unrelated to the immediately preceding verses. But if we keep in mind the literary structure of the chapter as a whole, we can well understand vv. 19-20 as referring to a prayer and a presence of Christ in his Church that have to do with reconciliation. The fraternal discipline that has been described is not a purely human administrative action. It takes place in a context of prayer that may have already become a set part of the early liturgy by the time the first gospel was composed. Moreover, the action of the brothers and sisters can expect assistance and ratification from the risen Lord. The words "two or three" may refer to a prayer uttered by two or three of the brethren who are officiating at an assembly of the community. The invocation of the name of Christ in Christian communal prayer played an important role in primitive Christian worship at a very early date.[12]

"Lord, how often shall my brother sin against me, and I forgive him?" (vv. 21-22). Matthew shifts here from a public sin that disturbs the Church (v. 15) to a private sin against a brother or sister (v. 21). He can make this transition because in his Church an offense against an individual and a rejection of community discipline are closely connected. Every sin against a brother or sister weakens the community and vice versa. We may note once again that the theme of forgiveness plays an important part in Matthew. For example, "If you forgive men their trespasses, your heavenly Father also will forgive you; but if you do not forgive men their trespasses, neither will your Father forgive your trespasses" (Matt 6:14-15; see also 9:5-6; 12:31-32; 18:23-35, the parable of the unforgiving servant;

26:28). Individual Christians, like the Christian community as a whole, must grant forgiveness over and over; this forgiveness knows no limits. Fraternal forgiveness now replaces the social imperatives of vengeance.

The general message of this chapter in Matthew sheds a good deal of light: all Christians must help one another; they must take care of the helpless and of sinners. They have an obligation to come to the aid of sinners and to do it prudently and without grinding them down. This duty is incumbent on the body of Christians as well as the pastor, because both sin and reconciliation have a community dimension.

John 20:20-23

The general sense of the passage seems quite clear: Christ has given his Church a mission and, with the mission, all the powers it needs for carrying it out. Jn 20:23 explains this power insofar as it takes form in the absolution of sins. According to some exegetes, the text is simply a variant derived from a prejohannine tradition and giving Matthew 18:18 a more specific application.[13]

We may see in this passage a confirmation of what was said above. According to John, the function of forgiving sins is entrusted to the *disciples*. Once again: should we identify these disciples with the Apostles? or with the entire Church, along the lines of what St. Paul says?

Those who hold that the disciples are in fact the Apostles have but a single argument: "Now Thomas, one of the twelve, . . . was not with them when Jesus came" (v. 24). Therefore, the group was made up of the Apostles. However, as a matter of fact, St. John has little to say of the "eleven" Apostles in his gospel (see 6:6-8; 13:5, 22). Moreover, the context is significant: "As the Father has sent me, even so I send you" (v. 21). It seems clear that Jesus is here addressing all Christians; the verse on forgiveness, therefore, should likewise refer to all Christians. "Receive the Holy Spirit": this gift of the Spirit is given to all who follow Jesus, as he indicates when he says, "He who believes in me, as the scripture has said, 'Out of his heart shall flow rivers of living water.' Now this he said about the Spirit, which those who believed in him were to receive" (Jn 7:38-39).

The role Jesus is here conferring is given, then, to the entire Church, that is, to the community of Christians. Salvation comes from the risen Christ who, due to the action of the Spirit, lives in the Church.

James 5:16-20

The Church has long appealed to this text in support of her power to forgive sins; in fact, she even gave it priority over the other two texts. Today there is much less frequent reference to the text, and the references made are more cautious, since the passage is speaking only of Christians who are ill.

It must be acknowledged, of course, that v. 16 – "Confess your sins to one another" – calls for the confession of sins – but for a mutual confession. Of greater interest is the connection we find here once again between prayer and the action of the elders. In my opinion, this passage of St. James confirms what I have already said: the letter is repeating that the forgiveness of sins is unintelligible apart from the saving intervention of Jesus, who is living now in his Church. The prayer of the just person wins forgiveness from God.

Conclusion

At the end of this analysis certain conclusions stand out. I shall summarize them briefly.

1. The ministry of reconciliation has been entrusted to the Church. Even if strict exegesis does not allow the shortcut that the Council of Trent takes in dealing with the transmission of the power of forgiveness that Jesus conferred on the Apostles after the resurrection, it remains true that the ministry of reconciliation has been entrusted to the Church: "God . . . through Christ reconciled us to himself and gave us the ministry of reconciliation; that is, God was in Christ reconciling the world to himself, not counting their trespasses against them, and entrusting to us the message of reconciliation" (2 Cor 5:18-20). As a group, the texts we have been analyzing confirm this; the general fact that the Church plays a part in the forgiveness of sins is quite clear.

2. This ministry, which is based on the terms *bind and loose* (it is

one application of this concept) and has been given by Jesus to his disciples, is an exercise of some kind of authority over sinners in the Church. Its effects reach into heaven; the ministry is therefore connected with the definitive struggle against evil. In addition, the function is a comprehensive one, knows no limitations, and is exercised in the daily life of Christians. Its ecclesial exercise requires the presence of a visible mediator who gives visible expression to the dialogue between sinners and Church. If this dialogue is to take place, sinners must exteriorize their desire for conversion, while the Church must give expression to the promised mercy and forgiveness of God. The Church is thus the locus of reconciliation.

3. In practice, the concrete manner of exercising this ministry need not have been established and determined in detail by Jesus himself, especially since a prechristian form for it already existed in the Judaism of the time. This involved the community visibly separating itself from the sinner, who has accepted the mastery of the Evil One. The sinner becomes "a Gentile and a tax collector" in the Church's eyes. But once the sinner repented, peace and communion were re-established; the sinner was thereby rescued from bondage to the Evil One and his or her sins were forgiven.

4. Finally, we can now see much more clearly the individual and communal dimensions of the ministry of reconciliation. The ministry is no longer directed simply to the individual. It does help sinners to acknowledge their sins and be converted, but it also urges a grasp of the communal aspect of both sin and reconciliation. Christians, living as they do in the Church, may not forget that their defects, if yielded to, have harmful repercussions on the group as a whole. Consequently, the community as a whole must take part in the reconciliation of sinners. Finally, and most importantly, the sacrament of reconciliation, like all the other sacraments, is an act of Christian faith in the salvation wrought by Jesus Christ. It is for this reason that the sacrament builds up the Church.[14]

3

The Values of Reconciliation in the Experience of the Church

How has the Christian community through the ages understood the scriptural texts I have been recalling? What has been its experience of forgiveness? We are in for a surprise at the very beginning: in the apostolic age the young Church seems to have no interest in developing what we now call a penitential rite. The texts of the Gospel that we regard as so clear and straightforward are perhaps not quite as persuasive as we like to think.

And yet it is certain, despite the silence of the first centuries on a specific penitential rite, that the early Christian communities did indeed experience the forgiveness of God. The penitential psalms, which show with what depth and sensitivity the Jewish soul experienced repentance, were also the preferred prayers of Christians when the time came to express their own feelings of penitence.

It was under the egis of the joyful experience of salvation that the sense of repentance evolved in Israel and that Christian penitence was born. Since the God of Jesus Christ is not other than the God of Abraham, and since sinners are sinners whether under the rule of grace or under the rule of the Law, it is not surprising to hear both John the Baptist and Jesus uttering threats that recall the violent rebukes of the prophets: "Unless you repent you will all likewise perish" (Lk 13:3, 5). Repentance remains so essential that the Lord's preaching ministry opens with a call to repentance and ends with the order that "repentance and forgiveness of sin should be preached in his name to all nations, beginning from Jerusalem" (Lk 24:47).

Yet, fearful though these threats were, the dominant mood in the Christian experience of repentance was one of trust. The fact that such emphasis is put on such parables as the prodigal son (Lk 15:11-32) and on such historical incidents as the woman who sins and repents (Lk 7:36-40) or the paralytic (Lk 5:17-26) are signs that leave no doubt. Thus it was with great confidence but without any naïveté that the early Christians professed the forgiveness of sins.

How did the institution of penance operate in the apostolic communities? It is hard to say. The point that is clear is that baptism brings the forgiveness of sins — "Repent, and be baptized every one of you in the name of Jesus Christ for the forgiveness of your sins" (Acts 2:38). But we do not see forgiveness also associated with a special rite, despite the clarity (as we see it now) of such texts as Mt 18:18-20 or Jn 20:21-23 that we just examined. In fact, the harshness used in speaking of the sins of the baptized — "For it is impossible to restore again to repentance those who have once been enlightened, . . . if they then commit apostasy, since they crucify the Son of God on their own account and hold him up to contempt" (Heb 6:4-6; see also 10:26-27) — seems to exclude recourse to another rite for a further forgiveness after baptism.

This really surprising contradiction can be seen at work in the dialectic that marks the lives of Christians in the early centuries. It is also of interest to see how, given these perspectives, the people involved in pastoral care dealt with the situation. The Letter of Clement of Rome (first century), while carefully showing the depth of religious life among the Christians of Rome, also contains a fervent appeal for conversion.[1] The *Letter of the Twelve Apostles* (second century) suggests a means which we nowadays call (with a touch of irony) fraternal correction: "If your brother sins against you, go and tell him. . . ." (Mt 18:15).[2]

At the same period, however, we do see the beginnings of a rite. It is presented timidly in the guise of a vision in *The Shepherd of Hermas* (ca. 140–150). This text must be read in order to see that the main elements in the rite that Tertullian will describe later on are already present. These are: the proclamation of the word; the repentance in which Christians acknowledge their sinfulness, determine to change not only their views but their way of life, and submit to mortification; the mercy of God. At the same time, a limit is set that is an expression of divine mercy and the serious quality of the repentance: Hermas proclaims a new chance for penance, but only one; otherwise there is no forgiveness after baptism. The principle of a *single* chance for repentance will be maintained for five centuries.[3]

From this time on, the Church will in fact have three forms of "sacramental" penance, even before introducing the term. Let us look at these forms and try to discern the values and benefits the Church saw in her various experiences.

1. First form: Canonical penance (third to seventh centuries)

While a penitential rite of some kind seems already to have been accepted in the second century, it is only in the third that we find an established ritual by means of which Christians can express their repentance. We may call this rite canonical because its details are prescribed in the canons of the Church.

Two chief concerns may be seen at work in the Church of the early centuries: that sins be submitted for penance, and that the community play a part in conversion and penance.

The famous controversy involving Tertullian, then a Montanist, and St. Cyprian shows a well-defined concept of the Church's penitential rite.[4] The question being asked in the third century was not so much which sins should be submitted for official penance, but whether the Church can receive sinners back no matter what sins they may have been guilty of. Two points call for special attention: the return of apostates and the forgiveness of adulterers.

Whatever be the truth about the episodes involving adulterers and apostates and whatever the varied interpretations given of them, one thing is certain: either the Church was opening the door to adulterers and apostates under the pressure of circumstances, or this kind of readmission was nothing new but simply a continuation of what had been done in the past, although not on so wide a scale, with the Church recognizing her duty of accepting all sinners of whatever kind. But this means that the rigorism of the texts in the Letter to the Hebrews had already been much reduced in the pastoral practice of the Christian community.[5]

The second main concern of the early Church was with the question of who was to exercise the ministry of reconciliation. In this matter, there was a factor making for confusion: the intervention of the martyrs (those who had suffered for their fidelity to their faith). Thanks to this intervention a number of apostates believed they could return to the Church without performing the required penance.

We should avoid giving too narrow an interpretation to the value placed on such interventions by the martyrs. We may say, however, that despite her special veneration for the martyrs as full-fledged imitators and therefore perfect followers of Christ, the early Church remained quite consistent with herself. The martyrs evidently deserved special veneration, but only the bishops, as the leaders responsible for the Church, had authority to decide on admission into the ecclesial community.

A description of the penitential rite of the time

Even though the rite was intended to show forth the merciful concern of the Lord, it was marked nonetheless by great severity. Tertullian's treatise on penitence already sketches for us the main stages in the conversion of sinners,[6] but it is in the writings of St. Augustine, bishop of Hippo (396–430), that we see all the implications of the process.[7] The synthesis he gives us reflects the practice current from the fourth to the seventh centuries.

The canonical rite had three main stages.

a) Admission

It was demanded that sinners acknowledge their sins before God and one another. This "confession" must be understood as meaning precisely an acknowledgment of a state of guilt; that is, sinners had to create in themselves the dispositions needed for a genuine confession. We are unable to say just how this "confession" was made. It seems that there were several ways. Someone might be condemned in the civil court for practicing magic or for homicide; the bishops then followed this with an ecclesiastical excommunication. There might be a more or less spontaneous self-accusation by the sinner; or an accusation more or less elicited by a sermon describing the sinner's situation, or the crime of an unworthy communion.[8] We presume too much if we presuppose a personal self-accusation to the bishop during the time before admission to penance; I have found no text that explicitly says this. Augustine's statement that he found himself in the presence of sinners whose sinfulness he knew need not be understood as referring to such a prior self-accusation.[9]

Admission to penance was a public act that took place in the presence of the gathered faithful. Public self-accusation does not seem to have been a general custom; St. Leo the Great (ca. 450) categorically rejects it.[10] The public accusation required for canonical penance cannot have included a detailed confession of sins. It was simply an expression to the Christian community of the will to be converted. Only this accusation was needed if the community was to reach out to these sinners, support them during their public penance, and bring them to the divine forgiveness that would find expression in the communal reconciliation on Holy Thursday.

b) The order of penitents

Before pronouncing the words of reconciliation the bishop admitted sinners to the *order of penitents,* a state characterized by exclusion from the liturgy and the imposition of severe penances. The rite of admission included a laying on of hands by which the blessings of God were invoked for the mortifications the penitents would endure. The gesture of laying on of hands meant that the light of the Gospel was shed on the life of these baptized individuals. By entering this order penitents acknowledged their alienation from God; now the words of the bishop aroused in them the desire for conversion.[11] Prayers accompanied this gesture of conversion in the Spirit. According to Jungmann, these blessings of the penitents later became the *oratio super populum* ("prayer over the people") during Lent. The congregation, too, prayed for the penitents during the "prayer of the faithful." Finally, the penitents never received Communion.[12]

Penitential exercises were imposed for different reasons.[13] They serve to express externally the fact that God's judgment was being warded off. They were also a solemn plea for the intercessory prayers of the faithful.

The element of infamy was present but was secondary. Penance was first and foremost the external sign of good dispositions in sinners who had not succeeded in being faithful to their baptism. Understandably, then, the rite of penance was called a second baptism or a baptism of pain. In any event, this penance was the last one possible for a Christian.

c) Reconciliation

Reconciliation restores access to the Eucharist, that is, to a full life in the Holy Spirit. It is completed by an imposition of hands amid a certain solemnity. Two points deserve attention in connection with the laying on of hands. The first is that part of the bishop's act of forgiveness was fervent intercession by both the bishop and the assembly, somewhat after the manner of the prayer *Passio Domini* that used to be prayed in the rite of penance.[14]

The second point is that reconciliation meant not only readmission to the juridical, visible community of the Church but also God's forgiveness of the sins. In short, the reconciliation was what we today would call sacramental.[15]

An impasse

The penitential discipline of the early centuries was geared only to a small number of Christians: those for whom the pledges made in baptism were a sacred commitment that had been made after mature reflection and was faithfully observed, sometimes at the cost of life itself. But when people entered the Church en masse, the gain in numbers necessarily meant a loss in quality. Consequently, it became increasingly necessary to take human weakness into account. We should have no illusions about the fervor of Christians, especially from the fourth century on. Many of the faithful whose sins obliged them to seek forgiveness brought with them the same kind of negligence as Christians in the same situation do today. This is why we see the Fathers of the Church preaching the obligation of repentance just as our modern preachers urge repentance on sinners today. However, the people of that former time were appalled at the thought of having to embrace the penitential state for the remainder of their lives. Rather than renounce marriage and any public offices they might have, they postponed conversion.

At the same time, however, and by a curious twist, penance underwent a development that is surprising, to say the least. It also became an exercise of perfection, as people had recourse to it not only for the forgiveness of serious sins but also for the sake of the merit attached to the penitential state. Just as at a later time, it was the devout rather than sinners who sought indulgences. Many embraced the penitential state just as others became religious, making no self-accusation except a general confession; to assure their perseverance, they sought connection with the religious orders and formed a new "class": the lay brothers (*conversi*).

In short, to become a penitent was equivalent to becoming a monk or priest. During this same period priesthood and religious profession were regarded as a second baptism. In consequence of this, clerics and religious were not admitted to the penitential rite. A serious sin meant reduction to the lay state: *non bis in eodem.*[16]

Given this state of affairs, it is not surprising that individuals should put off canonical penance until the end of their lives. Some synods even advised against imposing such penance on young people, for they would be forced to remain celibate.[17] To admit married people to it was to risk destroying the home. Never were regulations of the Church better observed. Canonical penance became more and more a preparation for death. If monks, religious, those already reconciled, the young and married could not have access to penance, then a sizable part of the community was excluded from the official penance of the Church.

If we think about it, this persistent severity is surprising. Tertullian had already complained that many drew back from the second baptism.[18] What would he have said a century later? During the early centuries of the Church's life no pastor would have seriously urged people to penance without placing serious restrictions. And yet the Christian community had to continue in existence. Moreover, many canonical prescriptions seemed to ignore the fact that people were avoiding penance. The Council of Nicaea (325) requires that Christians prepare for death by receiving viaticum.[19] The Council of Agde (506) obliges the faithful to receive communion three times a year; otherwise they are excommunicated.[20] St. John Chrysostom and St. Augustine both felt the failure of institutions to adapt themselves to the needs of souls. Thus St. Augustine says: "I exhort you to do penance. . . . I do not reprove you publicly because my aim is to heal and not to accuse."[21] And again: "Whoever knows the goodness of God . . . will be able to discern those who are not to be forced to do painful penance, even though they admit their sins."[22]

How did pastors in those days solve the problem? We can suggest worthwhile hypotheses but of course they are hard to prove. Vogel sees the situation of many at that time as being identical with the situation of sinners who find themselves forced to receive Communion without being able to go to confession first.[23]

The thirty-third canon of the Council of Châlon is also to be regarded as contributing an answer to the question just asked when it recalls the fact that confession to God alone, without the mediation of the Church, is always possible.[24] This is not an isolated text. In the early Church as also during the High Middle Ages and even in the penitential books, the confession of sins to God alone was never challenged. It would be easy to cite many witnesses for this statement. The principle of the confession of sins to God alone in the secret of one's conscience would be challenged only beginning in the eleventh century, as can be seen from the forgery cited by Burchard of Worms (1025), who attributes it to the "saints."[25]

2. Second form: Tariff penance (sixth to tenth centuries)

The earlier period was dominated by very strict requirements and by a consciousness of God's justice. The sixth century shows a growing sensitivity to God's mercy, in the measure that people become more clearly aware of the spiritual nature of the effects obtained by penance. But at the same time that the idea of penance is interiorized and the drama of conscience takes priority over the sense of guilt, canonical penance also gives way to individualized penance.

One of the first witnesses to this greater sensitivity to mercy is Caesarius of Arles (bishop from 503 to 542). His chief originality is in having "arranged" the penance granted to the dying in such a manner that it conformed to the old laws governing penance while at the same time it brought spiritual profit.[26]

The origins of the new form of penance are obscure. All that is left to us, after all, are some unique books called the penitentials[27] that take the form of lists, or tariffs, of penances. They are meant for the use of confessors, and they tell us what goes on at this period and henceforth in the private dealings of penitent and confessor. Custom was making it necessary to set a value, as it were, on the sins of the individual. This kind of penance responded better to the desires of Christians who were becoming increasingly focused on the cultivation of the interior life and therefore more conscious of the spiritual significance of penance than of its social implications.

The Irish Church seems to have been the first to make these new concessions; next came the Church of Great Britain. Here we find neither public penance nor solemn reconciliation. Instead we see the Church weighing guilt and imposing works of penance that were proportioned, in length and severity, to the sins committed. This is the system we now call "tariff penance." The practice of it soon became common across the continent.

The first explicit statement we have regarding it is from the Third Council of Toledo (589): "In some churches of Spain, contrary to canonical form, some individuals have developed the bad habit of doing penance for their sins and asking the priest for reconciliation each time they have sinned" (Canon 2). The Council rejects this practice as a "detestable abuse."[28]

At this point it is already a matter of *custom* and not simply of isolated instances. We may therefore infer that the custom goes back to still earlier times in an effort to meet a need which the Fathers of the fifth and sixth centuries were already pointing out.

The rigorous view of the Council does not seem to have produced results, since hardly fifty years later the eighth canon of the Council of Châlon officially approves the new practice: "With regard to penance, the medicine of the soul: we acknowledge its benefits to human beings, and since it is priests who assign penance to penitents once the latter have confessed their sins, all priests should willingly perform this office."[29]

Tariff penance will continue to be popular into the Carolingian period.[30] We should note, however, that the Fathers of the sixth century were still very much aware that penitents had to have the proper interior disposition for reconciliation.[31]

Analysis of the tariff form; a new impasse

We may begin by noting that this new formula for penance kept all the component elements of canonical penance: the accusation of sins, the request for and acceptance of penance, the performance of works of satisfaction. The minister of the Church continues to be the judge in this abbreviated process, but his role is at the same time significantly enlarged. Not only must he know whether to grant or refuse penance; he must also weigh the number and gravity of the sins in order to assign to each a penance that will insure its forgiveness.

Once the practice of exclusion had disappeared, thereby leaving reconciliation meaningless, there was no longer any reason for receiving and giving penance only once. The role of the bishop became extremely limited, and the administration of penance became increasingly a priestly function. Since the penitent was no longer excluded from the life of Christian society, he or she could, even before finishing the penance, receive the other sacraments again, except at times for a more or less lengthy privation of the Eucharist. Certain especially serious crimes, being infamous, would continue to bring with them a stricter penance; these sins would be the "reserved sins" of a later time. Tariff penance, which extended to every type of sin, necessarily required a secret accusation to the priest; thus the way was prepared for the sacramental seal or obligation of the priest to preserve absolute secrecy; at the same time, the internal forum and external forum became increasingly separated in juridical practice.

Attractive though tariff penance was, two difficulties soon arose. The first sprang from human weakness. According to the gravity of the sins, penitents would receive a more or less lengthy and more or less severe penance according to a fixed list, although the sinful act might be evaluated quite differently in different books, depending on the line taken by the penitential in question.

The penance or satisfaction was cumulative and since it could vary from a matter of days to a matter of years, it might well seem excessive by comparison with the length of a human life. Faced with the difficulty of performing a lengthy penance, some penitents might never return for absolution. Others were more ingenious and, with the merciful connivance of the Church, invented stratagems to solve the problem. They might have recourse to *redemptions,* that is, to shorter but harder penances in place of longer but less difficult ones; or to *compositions,* that is, the payment of a sum of money in place of the mortifications imposed; or to *substitutes,* that is, having others perform their penance for them (a lord obliged to fast for 300 days would have 300 serfs each fast for one day in his stead). (We may note in passing that we have here a partial source of the recourse to indulgences that would flourish in later centuries and would lead to new insight into the communion of saints.) There was nothing inherently reprehensible in these subterfuges, but it is easy to see to what abuses they could lead.

The second difficulty sprang from the variations between penitentials. This difficulty had already been foreseen in the ninth century, when the Council of Tours (813) had observed: "Since all the bishops have come together in our imperial palace [at Tours], we thought it necessary to decide precisely which of the ancient penitentials it would be better to follow."[32] These collections had originated in different circles and had had different categories of penitents in mind; as a result they multiplied with seemingly nothing in common between them except their ultimate purpose.

The Council of Châlon (813) decreed that the penitentials be eliminated and that there be a return to the ancient practice.[33] As we can imagine, this conciliar decree was a dead letter from the outset. In 829 the Council of Paris called for the burning of the penitentials.[34] But only in the eleventh century would Gregory VIII succeed in getting rid of them completely.

Tariff penance was quite rigorous in the beginning, like the discipline that it replaced, but it soon became milder and finally disappeared.

3. Third form: The private rite (from the eleventh century to today)

It can be said that by the eleventh century tariff penance had by and large ceased to exist in its typical form, that is, involving the use of the penitentials. Satisfaction was still required but now its determination was left to the confessor's discretion; the time-gap between accusation and absolution narrowed, and soon absolution was given before the performance of the penance. With this, we have reached the stage of private penance with which we are familiar today.

Origin

Here again, it is difficult to assign a precise date for the introduction of this new rite. The process by which new rituals were introduced was completely different then than now: at that time the Christian community lived its life, developed and changed; only then did authority intervene to pass new laws and legitimate the development.

The events described above led naturally to a combining of "confession" and "reconciliation," or accusation and absolution. We are told as much in Canon 31 of the *Statuta Bonifatii* (toward the end of the eleventh century): "Each priest will be sure to reconcile each penitent immediately after hearing his or her confession."

We can say that very soon after this time the practice became more widespread. We must not think, however, that the rite quickly attained the popularity it had among us twenty-five years ago. Private penance was a custom that did spread, but quite slowly. Alain of Lille (ca. 1200) complains that laypersons and even clerics confessed only once a year.[35] We need not be surprised, then, to find the Fourth Lateran Council, at the beginning of the thirteenth century, making it obligatory to go to confession at least once a year.[36]

Development of a doctrine on penance

This third phase does not start out as a different way of practicing the penitential discipline. The emphasis was rather on developing a theory in the light of purely speculative concerns. The writings of the thirteenth- and fourteenth-century Scholastics had a major and indeed decisive influence on the entire later system of Catholic theology. If we want to evaluate their work correctly in the area of penance, we must not isolate it from the system as a whole and especially from the sacramental theology of the period.[37]

It is easy to imagine the impact such a perspective had on the confessional accusation of one's sins. The minister is still the bishop or a priest who, because he has the care of souls or because he has been delegated by competent authority, has the necessary juridical powers. It is his function to evaluate the sins, impose penance by way of satisfaction, judge the dispositions of the penitent, and grant or refuse absolution. The accusation must therefore include all mortal sins and will profitably include other, lesser sins. Very early on, use was made of a familiar gospel image, and the "power of the keys" came to designate the Church's authority over the faithful in both the internal and the external forum (Mt 18:19).

The Church locks herself into a fixed position

The doctrine took a fixed form at the Council of Trent. Unfortunately, this fixed position was adopted under the pressure of circumstances and took a polemical form that was hardly geared to answering sensitive questions in an area of theology and practice that is especially complex.

Preoccupied as it was with defending the prerogatives of the priesthood, the Council stood fast on the *juridical* character and *ex opere operato* effectiveness of the priest's action in the sacrament. On the other hand, the lengthy and detailed chapters that the Council devotes to the acts of the penitent make it crystal clear that it has not lost sight of the interior conditions required for a Christian repentance. In fact, the Council did not even simply restate these, in opposition to a doctrine that reduced repentance to interior attitudes and nothing more; the Council went further and showed the need of contrition and a firm resolution in place of a faith marked solely by a barren timidity and terror. The attitudes that the Council calls for are those of a sincerely repentant sinner; their sincerity is gauged by the readiness they show to submit to the good pleasure of the offended Friend.

This was a theology born of conflict; the Church would have to wait until the twentieth century to move away from polemics and reach a more vibrant and vital conception of penance.[38]

Conclusion

This overview of the penitential rite in the Church's history may have been sketched a bit hastily. It does, however, enable us to get a better grasp of the aspects or dimension of Christian reconciliation.

The personal aspect

We note, first of all, the emphasis which all forms of penance place on *conversion*. Whatever the rite in favor at a given time, it must lead to or express a real conversion; otherwise it is a sham. Reconciliation in the Church is not a magical rite for putting order into our little personal matters of conscience or those of the institution. It it not enough simply to show that the sacrament of penance is necessary for the forgiveness of sins, for without conversion the sacrament makes no sense. The Lord needs us in order to make his salvation a reality in us.

The early centuries emphasized the *necessary role of prayer* in the process of divine forgiveness; in this they were at one with Scripture and its many references to such prayer. Conversion is not a matter solely of personal effort; God's initiative is indispensable. We can therefore be happy to see the new ritual stressing the need for the priest to pray with the penitent and with the repentant Church.

The social aspect

The *ecclesial dimension of sin* is one that was pretty much neglected in the penitential rite that most of us knew for only too many years. It is a dimension that must be recovered if the sacrament is to have its rightful social character. It was to help us realize that the mutual forgiveness of Christians, as made present and operative in the sacrament by the priest, is indeed something real. The priest is, first of all, the minister of the community of believers.

Finally, the sacrament of reconciliation is a sign of our *joyous hope* of sharing in the salvation that Jesus Christ has made a reality. The penitential rite is certainly a rite of forgiveness, but it is also and above all the Church's celebration of gratitude to God the redeemer.

II

The Dimensions
of Christian Reconciliation

4

The Need of Conversion

The penitential rite is to be seen as a complex act that may be understood as having different levels. One important function of the sacrament of reconciliation is surely to lead the Christian to a genuine conversion (the personal dimension) and to make him or her fully a member once again of the Church in which Christ, living in the Holy Spirit, continues to take flesh (the communal dimension). The sacrament thus becomes a living expression of faith in the salvation that has become a reality in Jesus Christ.

The call to conversion is evident throughout the biblical tradition; it also rings unceasingly down the centuries and reaches the people of our day. The Lord's concern for sinners must normally be a concern that is shared by the entire Christian community, and the community must create in itself an environment that promotes the reconciliation of all people.

Unfortunately, as we have seen, the contemporary world finds it increasingly difficult to admit its sins; consequently, it is unable to give expression to a conversion of which it feels no need. As we have also seen, sacramental penance is a means offered to sinners (i.e., all members of the Church) of giving voice to their condition vis-à-vis the Gospel; by showing them how to proceed it also enables them to set out on the path of conversion. Part of this process is evidently the sacramental expression of God's forgiveness.

We have also reflected on the fact that this process normally takes place in community, with the priest no longer thinking of himself as someone possessing powers, but rather as a representative of the ecclesial community whose duty is to help Christians persevere on the path of repentance to which they committed themselves at their baptism. The Church thus becomes a mediator not only in the specific action of forgiveness but in the entire conversion process as well.

My purpose here is to dwell on the implications of *Christian conversion*.

1. Toward an understanding of sin

Few people today — but the same was true in the past — are eager to call themselves sinners. There is and has always been a form of repression characteristic of sinners: the repression that makes them forget a discreditable past. Our faults set in motion countless mechanisms of defense; if these are not kept in control, they lead to a rejection, pure and simple, of the fact that we are sinners.[1]

Clearly, it is not by way of a rational and theological definition of sin that we shall manage to explain a reality that Christians cannot deny. Sin is too much a continually present fact in the life of the Church, just as it is in the biblical tradition, for its presence to be forgotten today any more than in the past. The real problem is to acknowledge it.

We need only open to any page of a newspaper in order to see that people are hemmed in on every side. In every area, whether it be political, economic or social, they find themselves faced with impasses. In whatever direction they advance they find the way blocked by seemingly insurmountable obstacles. Even nature itself is for them no longer the sweet nurse who dispenses peace and tranquillity.

People are limited human beings who seek to transcend their limitations. Believing that they cannot succeed in such an effort, they seek substitutes in pleasure, alcohol, or, in a word, every form of escape. But these are all artificial paradises. One need only spend a few minutes in any bar or cocktail lounge and one will begin to wonder whether there are any poor folk left in the city after 10 p.m. Workingmen who during the day were struggling to maintain their buying power have money to waste after dark. But an alert eye discovers that appearances may be deceiving. People here are feasting in order to forget their true condition; they are living beyond their means in order to forget the privations they suffer;

they fraternize and step out in lively dances in order to forget that they have been beating their heads against the wall throughout the day.

There are limitations even within the recesses of the person. Recent psychological studies have taught us that we are not as free as we like to think we are. The existential approach to the person had already taught Christian anthropology to see freedom as "ensnared," and we no longer speak of "human nature" but rather of the "human condition," a phrase that has become something of a slogan since the publication in 1933 of Malraux's novel *La condition humaine.*

Dealings with primitives show us the kind of activity that imprisons the human person in a cycle of eternal repetition. More broadly and clearly, time and space prove to be the most crucial of our prisons. St. Paul's words come to mind: "We were slaves to the elemental spirits of the universe" (Gal 4:3). Christian revelation prophesies our liberation from this captivity. This does not mean, however, that salvation consists in a flight or deliverance from the laws of space and time. Salvation is rather to be identified with the risen Jesus, in whose humanity we continue to be related to the world, but to a world now transfigured.

By his love for people Jesus Christ frees them from the subjection to sin, the law and death that they had brought upon themselves. The freedom proper to the glorified Christ is offered to all; it becomes a reality in them in the course of their personal history and activity, thanks to the power and inspiration they receive from the Spirit of freedom who has been given to them.

Christian life is based on the gift of God to persons in Christ, with this gift of himself becoming an invitation for them to return to God in Christ. God establishes a relation with human beings that becomes the true meaning and ultimate fulfillment of their lives. Although God initiates this relationship, it must become real and find expression in life itself.

This life in the risen Christ has power to create new structures that are capable of doing away with purely human structures or at least diminishing their dominant influence. However, this process supposes a real life in Christ and not simply a juridical membership in him through baptism.

Such is the meaning of conversion, that is, of a positive response to the call of Jesus. Such is the whole meaning of the spiritual freedom the risen Christ bestows on us, with all the demands of self-transcendence but also all the present and eschatological hope that this life brings with it.

The Church, especially in the phase of second evangelization, wishes to help men and women in their effort to be, to develop, to achieve fulfillment. She does this by helping them rediscover true values and by offering them a symbolic rite which restores or reaffirms their relation to themselves, to God, and to his world.

This task is one that the community of believers has undertaken ever since the first centuries of Christian life. The community has constantly sought to adjust its sights, as it were, so as to eliminate life's ambiguities through a rereading of God's word in the light of everyday existence. Through the centuries the Church has inevitably advanced through a succession of leaps and plateaus, depending on the rhythm of human and historical development. It is this that explains the many shifts of emphasis in the celebration of the sacrament of forgiveness, a celebration that had a long history before it took shape in the canons of the Council of Trent.

We all have daily experience of our infidelities. Our problem, therefore, is not to identify and catalog them but to face up to them before God, as members of the Christian community that is the Church.

The fact that we are Christians does not exempt us from the human condition. We still experience ourselves as limited human beings. We still perceive both ourselves and the world we live in as ambiguous and limited. We feel limited in relation to ourselves, in relation to others, and in relation to the world, and since these relations also shape our relation to God, we also feel limited in relation to him.

A little reflection will remind us that even though we are Christians we can let ourselves be drawn in the directions our limitations wish to take us. In other words, even after Jesus has rescued us from our basic limitation, our aloneness, our isolation from God, we can still sin. "I do not do the good I want, but the evil I do not want is what I do" (Rom 7.19). Our condition is sinful and shows itself in infractions, faults, sins.

The real Christian meaning of sin can thus be grasped only within an interpersonal relationship of love. We must move beyond questions of punishment, the law, or self-fulfillment: the true sense of sin arises only within the conviction of God's love for us "even though we are sinners" (see Rom 5.8); he loves us "with our sins."

The Christian sense of sin, then, involves a person and specifically a person who loves us. Sin is essentially a religious concept. The better we understand God and his love for us, the better we will understand sin and transgression. The sense of God and the sense of sin go together. We will understand the sense of sin when we realize that it is something involving two persons who are engaged in a dialogue, in an intersubjective relationship.

Sin will then be seen to be a disfigurement of love. It will be seen as the "No" with which we can answer God's invitation to live with him in love, and as a decision to live without the life this love brings.

Guilt, then, involves a relation to some one: a relation to a loving person and not to a law or to punishment or to an ideal self. This is precisely why guilt can disappear in the acceptance of forgiveness. Sin proves to be something quite paradoxical when it is thus experienced within a relationship of love. We experience sin as something much more serious than we would have regarded it as being if we linked it only to a law; at the same time, however, we experience it as much less serious, precisely because a loving person forgives whereas a law is incapable of forgiving. Consequently, the least peccadillo can be felt as serious and desolating because it is committed against someone who loves us and whom we love. Yet we can be quite serene about the worst folly or the most serious sin, because we experience it from within a relationship of love to someone who forgives.

These thoughts perhaps raise more questions than they answer; at least they have the advantage of telling me that if I am to understand sin I must learn of God's love for me — the merciful love God shows me.

If I am to understand sin I must properly evaluate my relation to my neighbour as well as his or her importance in my relation to God. If I am to understand sin I must grasp the importance of the Christian community that bids me pause a moment and realize my limitations; I must also realize the part I play in the community as far as love of God is concerned. No conversion is possible without this acknowledgment of sin.

2. The story of a conversion

I am a sinner

"Have mercy on me, for I am a sinner!" This cry from the heart that we hear in the gospel story is provoked by a christological event: the words of Jesus, a miracle of Jesus, or even the longing for healing. In the case of the woman taken in adultery (Jn 8:3-11), the beginning of a conversion is due to the malice of the people roundabout: "Has no one condemned you? . . . Neither do I condemn you; go, and do not sin again." We too need an event, a sensible, historical rite that will turn the salvation accomplished in Jesus into a reality for us here and now. To accept this fact, to be willing to hear the words of the gospel and compare our own view of life with them is to allow Christ Jesus to work in us and renew us and our whole activity in him.

Given this kind of conversion as the context, a return upon our past is not the result of a morbid desire to inflict pain on ourselves. We would rightly prefer to seek the face of the Lord instead of attending to the shabby actions we have done. But the obscurity that veils the history of a person and of ourselves in particular, as well as our uneasiness about the future — this should indeed call for our attention. True courage does not consist in calling ourselves sinners; it consists in accepting the fact that we are indeed sinners, accepting the fact that this is the kind of person we have been, and then wanting to change it.

In a world entrusted to them as free and responsible but also interdependent human beings, Christians hearing the word of God are aware that they stand in need of conversion and repentance. "The kingdom of God is at hand; repent, and believe in the gospel" (Mk 1:15). These opening words in the gospel message of salvation for the world have lost none of their penetrating relevance for the contemporary Christian conscience. Christians may no longer feel a need of burying themselves under dust and ashes as a sign of repentance, but they do look beyond their sin itself to concrete gestures that will restore them to an authentically Christian posture in the struggle against evil in all its forms and in the positive effort to build a more human world. All this Christians do in the presence of God.

It is true that conversion supposes an uprooting, a break with something, a kind of separation: specifically a break with sin and all that sin presupposes and implies. But we break with sin only in order to unite ourselves with the living God whose love is made known to us by the death and resurrection of Christ. Conversion consists in turning to some one, as St. Paul says in preaching to the Lycaonians: "We . . . bring you good news, that you should turn from these vain things to a living God who made the heaven and the earth and the sea and all that is in them" (Acts 14:15). The entire life of faith, and conversion first and foremost, must be seen as intimately connected with "the last times." In this sense, those who have been converted look forward to the return of the Lord, because they realize that the final age or last times have begun with the death and resurrection of Jesus.

The reader will have observed that, without using the name, I have been speaking of "contrition," which is at the very heart of repentance. Following the Council of Trent, the new Rite of Penance defines contrition as "heartfelt sorrow and aversion for the sin committed along with the intention of sinning no more."[2] More concretely: contrition is a commitment of the human person that sets the sinner on the road to forgiveness.

"On the road": the phrase tells us that conversion does not take place in a single act; at least, it does not usually happen this way. To speak of conversion is to speak of a stretch of time; turning and developing a new lifestyle and new ways of acting take a certain amount of time. All things are possible to God, of course, but many Christians are unbelievably slow. Penance in the early Church was a long process; even after schedules of penances had come into use, the bishop (or priest) would send a penitent away, requiring that he or she give proof of a genuine turning to God. And yet nowadays we want everything to be over in an instant that is readily absorbed into our agitated everyday lives! Doubtless we must not return to the practices of the early Church, but the latter can still inspire in us a respect for the often wavering faith of people who are entering upon a conversion.

When persons have lived a life of sin, even profound repentance will not ordinarily make immediately and fully clear to them the values and blessings of moral freedom, still less the great justice such freedom brings. For this reason it often happens that a penitent's good intentions, while sincere, are still very imperfect and certainly not universal in scope. Only by means of the entire conversion process, and even then only gradually, will sinners overcome the moral semiblindness that prevents them from seeing that a particular action falls under their general intention to avoid sin.

It is clear enough that the human will, because free, cannot be transformed without its own consent and cooperation. Sin springs from an act of the will and cannot be overcome except by a new free act; the will must cooperate, it must change its direction. Such is the complex process sinners must undergo in their return to God.

But conversion involves even more, for it demands the acceptance of grace by the soul being converted. The paradox of autonomy and dependence reaches an extreme form in the dynamics of Christian conversion. We must will our conversion, but this very will is itself the fruit of grace. Reconciliation is not accomplished by sheer force; rather, people receive it as a freely given gift from a merciful God. In a world of frantic, breathless effort, where everything depends on being successful in the struggle to exist, this special character of conversion makes it something unique for mind and heart. In any case, for human beings who, like experienced workmen, are proud of being able to solve all their problems by themselves, the special character of conversion is not easy to understand and accept. Think of how it undermines their autonomy, their claim to be the shapers of their own lives!

Once again: the initiative in this entire process comes from God through his Son and his Spirit who transforms the heart of the person.[3] The new self is not produced by the individual but is the work of God. In the last analysis, it is God who converts the heart of the person. Once they are moved by the same Spirit and the same love that inspired Jesus throughout his life and inspire him now in his risen state, men and women are capable of working effectively for the personal and social revolution that will bring them into a deeper communion and thus hasten the coming of the kingdom.

In this context, the acceptance of pardon is indeed a liberation from the past but it is even more an acceptance of new responsibilities making possible both the carrying out of new plans and a surer commitment to the service of our fellow human beings.

There is a further aspect we must appreciate correctly. In addition to being an opening of the self to God and an acceptance of pardon, Christian conversion is a learning of that forgiveness (Mt 18:21-22; 6:14-15) which human beings must be able to exchange and share in a world that is divided by often bitter and cruel conflicts but that nonetheless yearns for reconciliation. This reconciliation, given in principle in Jesus – "For in him all the fulness of God was pleased to dwell, and through him to reconcile to himself all things, whether on earth or in heaven, making peace by the blood of his cross" (Col 1:20) – continues to be the object of active expectation on the part of Christians. In a spirit of hope of the Lord's gifts, the individual Christian, together with the entire Church, is exhorted to a constantly renewed conversion. Here is where the practice of reconciliation in the Church takes on its full meaning: the Church must be the place where reconciliation through divine forgiveness is visibly manifested.

This last statement already explains the necessity of confessing one's sins to the Church.

Confessing one's sins

I do not wish to undertake a full-scale explanation of the benefits of confession; others have done that before me.[4] I do think it important, however, to make a few remarks on the subject.

It must be admitted that when we are confronted with our sin, our instinctive reaction is to place a cloak of silence over it, to hide it within ourselves. But it will be difficult to rid ourselves of our sin unless we are willing to voice it aloud.

There is an even greater value to telling my sins to the community. Faith in my real liberation comes only from the effort to live this faith as one of many brothers and sisters; only this warrants my adhering to these values. The community obliges sinners to open themselves and to reject their sin, which is essentially a turning in upon the self and its supposed sufficiency but actual limitation; sin is a refusal of what may lie ahead. It is therefore important that we frequently ask ourselves: "What influence have my words and actions had on my milieu? Have I helped make the Church and its witness to truth something vitally alive and operative?" Christians who confess their sins remind themselves that as members of the Church they play a part in her mission of bringing light and truth to every area of life.

We may note in passing that the word "confession," with its biblical echoes, has quite different connotations from the word "admission." "Confession" expresses freedom in quest of liberation; "admission" implies constraint. The Church has doubtless never physically constrained anyone to an admission, as is so often done in modern states, but moral pressure has indeed been exercised to force admissions, and this was a source of harm to the Christian people.

The modalities of confession have varied over the centuries. We can even say that they will depend on the conception Christians have of their transgressions and sins. When sin is thought of as a transgression of law, the confession will usually focus on each transgression. If sin is seen as action contrary to a plan of Christian life, the sin is by that fact looked at in a different light; the aim of confession will be to express the nonconformity of one's actual way of life with the plan given in the Gospel. If we take as our point of reference a society so structured that it begets injustice, then we will think of sin primarily as collective sin; in this case, confession will focus on the awareness of personal responsibility for the collective state of affairs and on steps to be taken to remedy it.

The new Rite of Penance,[5] in continuity once again with the Council of Trent, defines confession in terms of admission or self-accusation, that is, "accusation of one's own postbaptismal sins to a competent priest, in order to receive forgiveness for them." The Council of Trent regards this accusation as "instituted by the Lord," and therefore as a matter of *divine law* and, consequently, necessary for salvation.[6]

We will be disappointed if, in our effort to understand this assertion, we turn to the scripture texts that the Council adduces, for it
accommodates these texts in a way the modern theologian finds
quite unconvincing. The argument from tradition is quite valid as
far as the general obligation of confession goes, but it is much less
so for the modalities of confession, since these have varied greatly
down the centuries. The properly theological argument the Council
uses is in fact of a juridical type; that is, it is based on a consideration of the sacrament as being an act of judgment. "It is clear that
priests could not pass such a judgment [whether to forgive sins or to
retain them] if they were in ignorance of what the sins were, and
that they could not be fair in assigning penances if the penitents
confessed their sins in only a general way."[7] The power to forgive or
retain sins can be exercised in a proper manner only if the one possessing the power knows the sins and dispositions of the penitent.
But these can be known only through self-accusation. However, this
whole argument is valid only if it is first accepted that sacramental
penance is the exercise of a power by a competent authority.

On the theological level, then, we have only an argument from
authority, but it is an imposing one: that we are dealing with a truth
of divine law, so that anyone who rejects it is anathema. We may
note in passing that the text of the new Rite changes the expression
of this basic idea.[8]

I could wish that the Pontifical Commission had evaluated the
work done in recent years, of which I have been giving some brief
idea. In any case, I think it increasingly rash today to regard the *accusation*, in the precise sense given the term by the Council of
Trent, as an essential part of the sacrament.[9] The essential matter
for Christians who approach the Church in order to receive God's
forgiveness is the effort at conversion in response to God's efficacious call. Like the biblical *metanoia*, this effort involves the entire
person and, in all its seriousness, manifests itself in an external, ecclesial manner in the process I have been endeavoring to analyze.
For this reason the confession of sins has a Christian meaning to the
extent that it is the sign and embodiment of the external, ecclesial
aspect of the sinner's effort at conversion. The accusation of sins is
required only to the extent that it is an effective manifestation and
embodiment of this conversion. Other manifestations may profit-

ably replace self-accusation in certain circumstances (I am thinking here of our present circumstances). At bottom, it is less the sins we list for God (who knows them better than we do) than it is we ourselves, the sinners, who come to meet the Lord within a forgiving community.

Recommitment to the Christian community

Of what value in the past were those absolutions hastily received after more or less camouflaged or routine accusations? That is a secret that must be left to the mercy of God.

Whether we like it or not, the term the Church has always used to express the idea of "reconciliation" has been "penance." We delude ourselves therefore if we look for liberation without commitment. The biblical tradition does supply, of course, a whole arsenal of texts that justify the appeal for an unconditional reconciliation without further ado. Jesus tells the paralytic only to take his pallet and go home (Mk 2:1-12). He tells the sinful woman only that she is free because of her great love (Lk 7:36-50). The adulteress is saved just in time from stoning and is then sent away without any further proceedings: "Has no one condemned you? . . . Neither do I condemn you" (Jn 8:1-11). And yet, despite these texts, the Church continues to require a "satisfaction," once reconciliation has been effected.

The history of penitential discipline shows very clearly the persistence of this attitude in the life of the Church. "To do penance" is not simply to play a passive part in a rite that is ascribed to Christ and has been established in the community of salvation which is the Church. No, to do penance means also that penitents give expression in their lives to their desire for a living participation in the mystery of salvation. From the very first centuries, even before a specific rite was made obligatory, Christians were called to the practice of more or less rigorous penances. Even before there was any reflection on the full significance or meaning of this expiation, the Church was convinced that God had willed and Jesus had made clear the necessity of such expiation. The first parents had to expiate their sin in the pain of childbirth and daily toil (Gn 3:16-19); Miriam paid for hers with an attack of leprosy (Num 12:14ff.), as did

David with the death of his and Bathsheba's child (2 Sam 12:13-14). Peter expiates for his betrayal with his bitter weeping (Mt 26:75).

And yet, while the demand for expiation is unchanged, there has nonetheless been a considerable development connected with it. The mild penances imposed today are a far cry from the penances in sackcloth and ashes that were practiced in the early Church. But this development does not justify the fact that the act of confession has grown in importance, becoming the main act of expiation and calling for penances that are more subtle and interior. No matter what its exterior form, the nature of satisfaction does not change. Perhaps, however, the very fact that penances have become so easy brings out more clearly the real dynamics of satisfaction, which ought to bring the person to a permanent state known as the virtue of penance.

The historical reason why the priest must impose a prudent and appropriate penance on the penitent is to be found in the structure of the ancient penitential discipline, for in that discipline the accomplishment of the satisfaction was the clear proof of the sinner's interior repentance and conversion. This situation held until the time when the two phases of penance (confession and absolution) were fused, with the result that nowadays we can perform our penance after absolution.

Today, however, we see more clearly that when people accept those sanctions for their sin that necessarily remain even after forgiveness has been granted, they should see them as being objectifications of sin within themselves and in society. The imposition of mechanical acts is not fully in keeping with satisfaction as thus understood. The real need is rather to counteract the specific nature of the sin committed; such an offensive against sin, like all genuine Christian asceticism, consists in dying with Christ to "complete what is lacking in Christ's afflictions for the sake of his body" (Col 1:24).

It would be difficult these days for people to understand satisfaction as "expiation." That is how Augustine liked to take it,[10] and his view was to have a long future, being repeated century after century and leading to the famous distinction between *reatus culpae* (guilt) and *reatus poenae* (punishment) that a juridical conception of things will take to extremes. The theory of indulgences will be based on it.[11]

Traces of this idea of expiatory satisfaction are to be found in the Council of Trent.[12] I regard it as unfortunate that the idea persists in the new Rite of Penance.[13]

There is nothing against conceiving satisfaction as being the process of the person's maturation, whereby all the energies of the human reality are gradually integrated into the free person's basic option. Satisfaction is not a kind of fine whereby we pay for God's forgiveness; nor is it a fine sinners have to pay in order to make even fuller a divine forgiveness that is already complete indeed but that, without the fine, would remain purely in the ritual order. No, satisfaction is a talent given us that we are to make bear a hundredfold fruit; concretely, it is our recommitment to the Christian life.

People have the privilege of giving a meaning to their own activity through the attitude they adopt toward the gospel; they also have the privilege of organizing both themselves and the world they live in and of placing on that world the seal of the values by which they choose to live. Precisely to the extent that they have the privilege and duty of structuring their own behavior and their own universe in accordance with evangelical values, they also have the right and duty of accepting responsibility for their own actions.

The moral actions of men and women spring not from freedom of an angelic kind but from a human freedom that involves even the most fundamental levels of their being. The latter condition freedom and are in turn conditioned by it. Consequently, just as all the levels or zones of affectivity, even the most obscure, are involved in sin, so they are elements in the person's situation of guilt.

In closing this chapter, let me put the matter more simply. When sinners set out on the road to conversion, their task does not end with the absolution of the priest. Rather, they must show that they are new creatures who are recommitted to the way of salvation, and that they accept this task each successive day. They will give evidence of this recommitment by a change in the way they live, and this is usually not easy; perseverance is even less easy. The Church reminds sinners of this fact especially at the moment of conversion: the penance the Church imposes is a means of launching them on the path of persevering change. Whether it be mild or severe, this penance, in addition to being a reminder, also makes clear to sinners that the Christian community is at their side on the road of liberation.[14]

5

The Power of the Encounter

Although the preceding chapter was concerned with the individual or personal aspect of the sacrament of reconciliation, I have made frequent reference to the fact that the process of conversion takes place within the Church. In the present chapter I intend to concentrate on this communal aspect of the sacrament. Following both biblical tradition and the early tradition of the Church, I shall first discuss the minister of reconciliation as being a representative of the Christian community. Then I shall go on to point out the conclusions that follow from this approach to the sacrament.

1. The pastor, a representative of the Christian people

God alone can forgive sin, but it is the Church that mediates that forgiveness. This is a basic truth of the Christian faith. Our concern here is with the way in which the Church carries out her function. In other words: What role does the priest play in the celebration of penance? Does he merely give solemn ratification of a forgiveness that sinners have already won by their personal efforts? Or, on the contrary, are sins (serious sins, at least) forgiven only because the priest intervenes? Nowhere in the documents that have come down to us is the question asked as plainly as I have just asked it. It must be said, however, that it has long been present, more or less confusedly, in the Christian mind.

When faced with the heresy that saw in penance a purely external ritual involving the sinner and the Church but no intervention of God, St. Augustine repeatedly affirmed that "without the prayer of the priests there is no forgiveness of sins. Ecclesiastical reconciliation, on the other hand, brings the restoration of favor with God. For in this great action Christ continually intervenes."[1]

Augustine did not, however, go very far in his analysis of the problem. The most he does is to try to shed some light on it with the help of an illustration that may, at first reading, strike us as amusing.

The act of "loosing" is illustrated from the story of Lazarus (Jn 11:1-43), the dead man whom only the voice of the Lord could bring back to life. Sinners who do penance have already regained life, like Lazarus, but they are not yet loosed; they will come forth from the tomb when the Church intervenes to release them. The role of the Church is to remove the bindings, to do for them what the disciples did for Lazarus. This shows us, right off, the necessity of being in the Church if our sins are to be forgiven. For Augustine, then, the justification of sinners is a work in which the Church plays a part.

Once confession and absolution were brought together in a single action, penance took on an external form that raised our problem in a somewhat new form. From this time on, the emphasis will no longer be on penitential works (satisfaction) but on absolution (a ritual gesture), even while contrition (conversion of heart) continues to be regarded as basic. Let me, therefore, rephrase our question in schematic form: sin can be forgiven only by God; conversion wins this forgiveness from God, at least if it is a perfect conversion (perfect contrition); what, then, is left for the absolution to accomplish?

I have no intention of reviewing here the many explanations offered by the theologians, especially those of the twelfth and thirteenth centuries, nor the kind of pious dispute that ensued between the contritionists and the attritionists. I prefer to let these sink into the forgetfulness to which the recent generation has consigned them.[2]

The modern mind does not know what to make of these rational, almost geometric demonstrations. The latter are explicable in the light of the historical development that led to them. The early Church was very conscious that God alone can forgive sin, and therefore she assigned herself only a *ministerium* or ministerial role. The Church represents the community of the redeemed. Only the

Spirit can forgive sin, but since the Church is the locus or embodiment of the Spirit, it is clearly only through communion with her that sinners can find peace with God. When the early Christians participated in penitential ceremonies, they regarded themselves as having both a receptive and an active part in the community that is assembled in the Spirit and by its intercession effectively wins forgiveness from God.

In the course of time, a new rite replaced the old. But while the later rite has evident pastoral advantages, it is also less meaningful. No longer does the entire ecclesial community take part in an action that ought to be a deeply moving one for the participant. Instead, the whole business takes place privately between the penitent and the priest who is the head of the community (which he sums up in his person, as it were), not by delegation but by a new quality that his ordination confers on him. The priest or confessor almost imperceptibly becomes a delegate of God because he is now the delegate of the institutional Church rather than of the Church as assembly of the faithful.

Consequently an onlooker sees in the penitential action only a confrontation between two human beings. Instead of a visible manifestation of divine love by the Church, we encounter simply a person endowed with power. Inevitably, he is asked to justify his claim to power.[3]

It is possible, however, to understand the role of the priest quite differently.[4] This understanding is based on the interpretation given of the texts of Scripture, especially those of Matthew and John; it helps us understand why the new Rite of Penance prefers to speak of the sacrament of reconciliation.

The biblical expression *bind and loose* does not refer primarily to a "right" of granting or refusing absolution,[5] but to an ability to exclude persons from the Christian community and to bring them back into it again.[6]

We have already seen that before being the work of a human being conversion is the work of God. We have also seen the importance and even the efficacy of prayer in the process of conversion. The prayer of the Church is the prayer of Christ himself who, as Mediator with the Father, obtains forgiveness for us. There is thus a twofold mediation: that of Christ and that of the Church. At the same time, the mediation is one because that of Christ incorporates that of the Church, gives it its power, and finds visible expression in it. Christ is "the sacrament of (the encounter with) God," or the primordial sacrament, while the Church is "the sacrament of the heavenly Christ."[7]

"Who can forgive sins but God alone?" (Mk 2:7). Very true, but "the Son of man has authority on earth to forgive sins" because this human being is, in his very person, the Son of God; he is God himself. Therefore, everything human in him — the mouth that speaks, the human mind that understands words, and the will that gives orders — acts spontaneously and freely under the egis of the divinity and in full harmony with it. Jesus the man is therefore the supreme locus of God's presence in the world as savior.[8]

In leaving the visible world Christ did not cease to be Lord of history; he dominates it, and does so by his presence. The Church is thus the locus and visible center of Christ's saving power as this is still at work in the world and will be until the end of time. In this context we might repeat St. Paul's words, "God was in Christ reconciling the world to himself" (2 Cor 5:19) and complete them as follows: "And Christ is now in the Church, offering to all human beings the reconciliation he won, once for all, on the cross."

The point of all this is to make it clear that Christ's power over sin is naught else than the power of God who *alone* can forgive sin, give grace, and restore life; and that the Church's ministry in turn is a ministry received from Christ. It is in this sense that the sacraments are said to be "actions of Christ," done in the power of the Holy Spirit.

With this we are back in the Augustinian perspective of an ascending mediation of the Son who intercedes with the Father (as in the story of Lazarus, Jn 11:41-42), since Christ alone, and not the priest, is mediator between God and the human race. This intercessory mediation, whether that of Christ as man or of the Church that is made up of human beings in whom Christ lives by the power of the Holy Spirit (a new incarnation of God), leads to the same end: "God alone gives grace."

Against this background we understand better how the priest acts as the representative of the Church, with the ministry of reconciliation being one of the Church's charisms. Once we adopt this standpoint, it becomes clear that only special historical circumstances could have led to an interpretation of the texts in Matthew and John in which the "disciples" were identified with the "apostles." In fact, the ministry of reconciliation belongs rather to the Christian community that exercises it through a president, a minister.

Now the real situation is clear: Christians who sin are members of the Church; therefore their sins against God are at the same time sins against the Church in and through which Christ lives. Reconciliation with the Church is not to be understood as something purely external, purely juridical and social, but rather as an effective new participation of these members in the Mystical Body of Christ, that is, in the vital communion – which the Church is – with the Father, through the Son, in the Holy Spirit.

It is the prayer of the assembly – but, clearly, an assembly that has a priest as president and leader – that causes the voice of Christ to ring in the Father's ears. At times, the priest may be alone when he fulfills his role of bearing witness to the conversion of sinners and of giving them the sign of forgiveness; nonetheless, by reason of the fact that he is a minister, he has the ecclesial community with him. We may therefore say with Poschmann as he comments on Augustine and Cyprian: The "proper holder [of the power of the keys] is the universal Church, that is the collectivity of its members who are animated by the Holy Spirit. Not Peter alone 'but the universal Church binds and looses sins.'"[9]

2. The consequences of this approach to the sacrament

In a sense, the place of the sacrament of reconciliation in the economy of salvation seems seriously undermined. This is to say: the need of this sacrament for obtaining grace and therefore for access to the Eucharist is no longer as clear as it was.

Theologians have long argued over whether the necessity of the sacrament of penance in the Church is of divine law or ecclesiastical law.[10] As a matter of fact, there is no completely cogent argument that might directly resolve the problem one way or the other. It is a fact, however, that in Scripture the sacrament is presented as the normal means of conversion in the Church.

a) *Means of reconciliation*

Justification involves two complementary steps. One is preparatory: sinners' awareness of their sinfulness, and their desire to return to God through participation in the mystery of salvation: "Therefore, since we are justified by faith, we have peace with God through our Lord Jesus Christ" (Rom 5:1). The other is justification itself that effects conversion because it is the grace of God. The growing intensity of human dispositions finally ends in conversion, the key component of which is a real participation in God.

When sinners acknowledge what they are, they are in a sense reconciled with themselves and, thereby, called to be reconciled to one another. This reconciliation in turn leads into reconciliation with God.

Taking what we have thus far seen, we can say that there is in Jesus Christ the possibility of a reconciliation with God that is not mediated by the sacramental rite. Inasmuch as this reconciliation takes place without the actual reception of the sacrament, it is produced as an immediate effect of the conversion that operates by the power of God's efficacious grace and in virtue of the Christian's baptism. Here we are in agreement with the Council of Châlon in 813:

> Some say we must confess our sins to God alone; others, that we must confess them to a priest. Both practices are current in the Church and both are the source of great benefit. We are therefore to confess our sins to God alone – God who alone forgives them – and we are to say with David: "I have made my sin known to you; I have not hidden my wickedness. I said: I wish to confess my transgressions to God, and you have forgiven my guilt and my sin" (Ps 31:5). On the other hand, according to the Apostle's instructions (see Jas 5), we are to confess our sins to one another, in order that we may be reconciled. Confession made to God alone cleanses us of our sins; the confession we make to priests teaches us how to cleanse ourselves of our sins. God, the author and dispenser of salvation and well-being, grants us forgiveness, at one time by the operation of his invisible power, at another by the action of the physicians of the soul.[11]

This is surely a remarkable text, reminding us that a "confession" made to God alone, without the mediation of a confessor, is always possible. Vogel adds: "It would be easy to cite many witnesses to the same effect." It is also clear that we find some of the Scholastic theologians adopting a similar position, especially the Scholastics of the Franciscan School,[12] and accepting that there are two ways to obtain the forgiveness of sins. The sacramental rite can therefore be obligatory only if it is made the object of a precept or institution of the Church.

This does not, however, reduce the importance of the Church's sacrament. If we understand the situation properly, we see that the sacrament plays a different but complementary role in the sinner's life.

First of all, in her rite the Church intercedes for sinners. If they have already attained to a genuine conversion, then they are already justified in Jesus Christ who has cooperated with them in their efforts. Human nature, however, weighed down as it is by these very sins, does not always succeed in attaining to the maturity of a genuine conversion. Then the Church acts through her priest who intervenes efficaciously with his prayer.

The penitential rite also provides penitents with the opportunity of admitting their sins to themselves and, through confession, admitting them also to the priest so that he may reconcile these penitents with the community of believers. Such a reconciliation is the first and principal effect of absolution by a priest. By their sins men and women separate themselves from the Church; they need, therefore, to admit these sins to the Church. The priest reconciles sinners to the Church, and this action becomes at the same time the sacramental sign of God's forgiveness.

We can go even further. If sin is an affront to the Church, it is also an affront to each member of the community. Each member of the community therefore must forgive and be reconciled to his or her brother or sister. The priest's gesture of reconciliation carries with it the forgiveness of all the Christians of a living community. Thus we come back to the deeper meaning of all those biblical texts that urge us to the mutual pardon so marvelously expressed in the Our Father: "Forgive us our debts, as we also have forgiven our debtors" (Mt 6:12).

There is an obvious objection to be raised at this point: "Not all Christians are so ready to forgive!" Granted! But the Lord's invitation is no less urgent on that account, and, besides, his mercy is great enough to transcend our weakness and mediocrity. That is what the parable of the Prodigal Son is telling us if we attend carefully to what the father says to his elder son.

This elder brother has to some extent been likewise hurt by his younger brother's escapade; we hear him resisting his father. The father does not challenge the son's reasons for being angry; he simply asks him to be understanding and forgiving (Lk 15:11-32).[13]

b) *The functions of the penitential rite*

We may now more easily distinguish two essential functions of the sacrament of reconciliation: in one, *the entire community* is invited to celebrate the gift of reconciliation; in the other, certain Christians ask the Church to celebrate with them the gift of *their* reconciliation.

In the Church, the invitation to celebrate the sacrament of reconciliation is evidently addressed to all Christians insofar as they are members of the Church. It is also addressed, but in a different way, to those who recognize that they have more or less radically cut themselves off from the community by a long period of indifference or by behavior that is clearly incompatible with the call to live according to the gospel.

This second function of penance requires no lengthy consideration; it has left its mark only too clearly on our manner of thinking about reconciliation. In fact, it has so influenced our approach to the sacrament that it has caused us to lose sight of the other, surely more basic function. Penance is a sacrament, that is, a symbolic action that expresses grace and makes it real among us. The action of the Church links the conversion of sinners to the passion of Jesus Christ for the purpose of bringing these individuals into vital union with God. But there is more to the sacrament than that.

Within the human race there is a group of people who call themselves the Church. Its members are not necessarily better than other people, but they are signs, efficacious signs of salvation for the rest of the race. We can make our way back to God only by becoming part of the sign of reconciliation which is the Church. Thus the sacrament of reconciliation is also a manifestation of the Church that constantly repeats to the human race: "I proclaim salvation to you." As for ourselves, we do not take part in the sacrament of penance only to get rid of our sins but also in order to proclaim to the world that there is salvation for sinners.

When we reach the point of admitting ourselves to be sinners, we are not first and foremost accepting another human being whose mission it is to absolve us. What we are doing first of all is agreeing to become part of this saving sign that makes salvation present to all of us. It would indeed be small-minded to think of the rite of penance solely as a means of getting ourselves individually out of the bad situations we put ourselves in and of gaining reconciliation with God. In fact, it is not even enough to speak simply of reconciliation with God and with the Church. We must go further and accept the fact that in this sacrament salvation is being offered to all men and women. That is, we must think of ourselves as being henceforth a sign to the world, the sign of the converted sinner. Such an approach is no longer the individualistic one of the sinner who commits a piece of folly and seeks to regain his or her innocence. It is rather an approach inspired by faith. Just as the baptized do not simply take part in a rite that saves them but become members of an institution that considers them now to be saviors of the world, so in the sacrament of reconciliation we enter an institution that will be the living proof that the sin of the world has been overcome.

On occasion, a local church invites its members to celebrate the sacrament of reconciliation. The more that Christians are really active members of the community and savor the gift of communion, the more they will feel personally addressed in this invitation and desirous of responding to it and joining their brothers and sisters in celebrating with joy the reconciliation, constantly needed and constantly offered, of the Church with her Savior.

It is important, therefore, that this reconciliation should be for us a Christian solidarity of us all as sinners, as well as a human solidarity with those who are not of the Church.

In this way the entire people of God who live within the covenant that is grounded in Jesus and his paschal mystery are used by Christ as an instrument for the redemption of the whole race. In this sense, the Church mediates the reconciliation that is God's gift, but she does so in Christ and through a ministry of reconciliation that she exercises. Let us read Paul once again: "All this is from God, who through Christ reconciled us to himself and gave us the ministry of reconciliation; that is, God was in Christ reconciling the world to himself, not counting their trespasses against them, and entrusting to us the message of reconciliation" (2 Cor 5:18-19).

If the entire Church plays a part in the forgiveness of sins, this is not simply, as we said above, because all sin affects society. It is also because of the structure or, rather, the nature of the religious relation: the gift of communion with God creates solidarity among people.

The Church is the fundamental, collective, institutional sacrament that by its very existence tells all human beings that they are already saved in Jesus Christ. At the same time she calls all these human beings to lay effective hold on salvation and reconciliation (which are always being offered) as a reality already existing and, at the same time, as an invitation to the utterly new.

Let us not hesitate to assert that there is in Jesus Christ a forgiveness of sins, a reconciliation, a liberation that are meant for the human race as a "body." The Church says as much to the human race because she herself is a "body." This is a forgotten truth but one that proves very fruitful as soon as we recapture it. If the Church formerly played so great a part in the reconciliation of sinners, and if she wishes to play a greater part in the sacrament of penance than she now does, she is not motivated solely by the desire to bring sheep back to the fold and to reconcile human beings with God. It is also because she wants to be reconciled as a Church, that is, as a sacrament that must convey to the human race the message that it is saved in Jesus Christ. For, in sinners who come back to the Christian community, the Church sees children who once went astray and who now, from their place in the world, will henceforth tell their fellow human beings that they are redeemed. They will seek to decipher in faith the signs of redemption that are present in the human race and its history, and will cause the Church to have a better grasp of her mission. "Nothing so deeply commits a human being as repentance."[14]

c) *The revitalization of "devotional confession"*

The function of reconciliation that we have just been discussing also reduces somewhat the importance of the distinction between mortal and venial sin and gives new meaning to so-called "devotional confession."[15]

The recognition that confession of devotion is possible is not necessarily an acknowledgment that it is also prudent. It has its opponents, and understandably. Many have claimed that it was deleterious to the spiritual life because it caused Christians to be preoccupied with their own guilt. The objection is a valid one. What value this kind of confession may have is not to be derived from a connection with personal sin. We know, moreover, that the Council of Trent,[16] following the entire tradition, asserts that everyday sins can be removed by many other means, among them the reception of the Eucharist.[17]

There are other, and surely more cogent, motives for confession of devotion. The sacraments are expressions of the life of the Church in which individual believers are incorporated into the body of Christ. Christians guilty of sin therefore celebrate reconciliation not only as people personally sinful (even if they are this to a greater or lesser extent) but also as members of a sinful Church whose mission it is to give the human race a visible sign of the salvation that has been accomplished in Jesus Christ and in which she truly believes.

Confession of devotion, then, can be fitted harmoniously and prudently into the overall pattern of the spiritual life. On one condition, however: that it not be repeated too often. The Church's experience makes it quite clear that repetition easily begets routine in human beings. And routine has never been proof of a deep faith.

What I have been saying in this chapter challenges a number of other positions long taken as obvious.[18] My observations on the liturgical rite in the following pages will provide an opportunity for some pertinent remarks.

III

The Forms of the
Penitential Rite

6

Let Us Be Reconciled

My intention in these final pages is to discuss the practical problem that the sacrament of reconciliation raises for pastors. The preceding chapters have provided worthwhile perspectives that will serve now as the basis for pastoral considerations. I shall also make use of the results of experiments conducted in the Canadian dioceses of the Inter-Montreal region in 1975. The chief document, however, will continue to be the new *Rite of Penance*.

Sacramental penance has for its setting a dialogue among Christians: a reconciliation of Christians with one another that becomes the *sign* or *symbol* of reconciliation with God. There is something special about this dialogue because it is Christic, that is, centered on Christ. It makes the God-man present in that it commemorates the history of the salvation that was accomplished in Jesus Christ. To this end, there must be present a minister who is charged with the mission of the Church and who in a public, ecclesial process establishes a link with the history of salvation.

A minister is required. At present, this minister is a priest, but a priest of a particular type, not because he has "powers" but because he is charged with the mission of the Church and presides over the Christian assembly.

Nor is the priest I encounter in this sacrament primarily a director of conscience. All the better if he is this, since such direction is a felicitous prolongation of confession. But it is not essential to the sacrament of reconciliation that the confessor be a good director. The important thing is that he is charged with a mission, namely, the proclamation of the world's salvation.

This status is now expressed in the term "jurisdiction." The bishop has the primary responsibility and shares it with others who support him in his pastoral activity. The theologians have endeavored with more or less success to explain the powers of *orders* and *jurisdiction* proper to the priest as confessor. The older manuals record these efforts at explanation.[1]

These explanations are perhaps not as important as people like to think. We need bear in mind only that the basic role of the priest is to assemble the people and that his power, if power it is, is a liturgical power. In the name of Jesus Christ and with and in him, the priest has the mission of gathering all human beings. He is the person who establishes relations within the Christian community.[2]

The minister, *in an ecclesial process, establishes a link with the history of salvation.* It is the word that makes this connection. This is another reason for preferring to the low whisper of the confessional a celebration in which we have time to read and share the biblical text. We all tend to turn in on ourselves while examining our consciences, whereas in fact it is God and not ourselves that we should be looking at. It is by focusing on God that we become aware of our wretched state and our sins. The first good news that the celebrant must proclaim is therefore the revelation that God loves us, that in the person of his own Son he even carries the sins of the world.

In light of all that I have been saying in this book, the penitential rite should show the following characteristic traits:

— It is first and foremost a *profession of faith.*

— It is a *place of prayer.* The Church first intercedes and only then pronounces a judgment.

— It is a *gesture of the Church* and not a reserved reception by a person who possesses power and is ready to forgive or condemn according to the dispositions of the penitent. The entire Church as a priestly people acts — different members in different ways — and carries on the work of reconciliation that God has entrusted to it (2 Cor 5:18). By the ministry of the pastor the Church herself acts as instrument of conversion and forgiveness.

— It makes it possible for *the penitent to measure his or her life against the word of God.* The rite needs, therefore, to be properly located once again in relation to the dynamics of Christian life as a whole.[3]

— It is a *reconciliation of Christians with one another* and thus a sign of their reconciliation with God.

In my view the new rite of reconciliation shows all these traits, and we should develop them with deep pastoral concern. Four types of celebration are offered to those in the pastoral ministry: 1) celebration with an individual penitent; 2) communal celebration with individual confession and absolution (I shall refer to this simply as "communal celebration"); 3) communal celebration with general absolution (I shall refer to this simply as "general absolution"); 4) nonsacramental celebration of penance.

Contrary to the superficial impression a first reading of the document might give, these forms are offered not as independent but as complementary, and it is this complementarity that I shall be emphasizing in the following pages.[4] In addition, the use of the new rite will be better assured of success if we take into account the real needs of the faithful and if our efforts are sustained and measured.

1. Individual absolution in a private rite

If the actions of priest and penitent are to become meaningful once again, it is important that we take all the time needed for doing them properly. We can never repeat often enough that the pastor and the faithful should not move on too quickly to the accusation of sins; this last can only profit from being properly located within a larger whole and from a good preparation.

The new rite makes some valuable points here and suggests a sequence of actions that will help private confession become a real celebration. Among other things, it suggests:

— a preparation of priest and penitent through prayer;

— the penitent is greeted as a brother or sister by the priest, who takes the time to address a few "human" words to the person. It will often be necessary for the penitent to make himself or herself known to the priest in a brief conversation;

— a recall of God's word in the form of a quotation or a short reading. The right passage from the word of God will not be as difficult to determine as many pastors still think. Once the priest gets to know the penitent sufficiently through the welcome and possible conversation that I just mentioned, he will have no trouble finding a passage from Scripture that fits the situation of the penitent. After these words from Scripture the priest asks the penitent to evaluate his or her overall Christian life in the light of the gospel and to specify his or her sins. Is there any better way of introducing new life into the examination of conscience?

— a time of prayer that should not be omitted. Should a pastor find it difficult to pray with the faithful?

— a somewhat extended formula of absolution that emphasizes the role of the Trinity in the reconciliation, as well as the place of the Church's ministry. An individual celebration should bring out the ecclesial dimension of penance, for it is by signaling the forgiveness of the Church that the priest makes known the forgiveness of God. He, the priest, conveys the forgiveness of the entire community and of each individual Christian. Penitents will thus be made more conscious of the need of that mutual forgiveness that a genuine conversion requires; as we pray in the Our Father, "Forgive us our trespasses *as* we forgive those who trespass against us."

All this care bestowed on the rite itself should not make us forget the necessity of a more remote preparation through adequate preaching. If the sacrament of penance is to regain its proper place in the life of the faithful, the first and at the same time the most difficult pastoral task is to proclaim the message of the Lord over and over: "Repent, and believe in the gospel" (Mk 1:15). The penitential seasons of Advent and Lent are especially appropriate times for this emphasis.

This first manner of celebrating the sacrament will make great demands on both pastor and penitent. Let us repeat again that it will only suffer if it is done in slapdash fashion. It is hard to imagine a return to the old sessions in the confessional, for as soon as a line of waiting penitents forms, it is practically impossible for the confessor not to speed up the confessions. Schedules must be arranged that make it possible to receive each penitent in a leisurely manner and in the best conditions for a carefully conducted celebration.

2. Individual absolution in a communal rite

When a number of penitents present themselves at the same time, it is better to prepare them all by means of a communal rite.

The pastor may also invite his parishioners to such celebrations.

A communal celebration becomes advisable not only due to the practical considerations of numbers and time that I have just mentioned, but also for the inherent advantages of this form: "Communal celebration shows more clearly the ecclesial nature of penance. The faithful listen together to the word of God . . . and help each other through common prayer."[5]

The immediate preparation of several persons for confession can thus be conducted in a more meaningful way, and certainly more easily, if it is done in common. But all necessary care must be taken with the reading from the word of God, the homily, the examination of conscience, and the common prayer, according to the scheme proposed in the new ritual.

While it is important that great care be devoted to this first or communal part of the celebration, equal care must be given to the individual's meeting with the priest. The rite would lose a great deal of its value if it were regarded simply as a way of quickly getting through the required detailed accusation. It seems to be a rather widespread practice in these celebrations to urge penitents and confessors to carry out this private part of the rite in a summary fashion, the penitents being explicitly asked to limit themselves to a dry list of sins, and the confessor to give absolution without adding any personal exhortation. Such a procedure can only intensify the element of the mechanical for which individual confession has often been blamed. It can only accentuate the contrast between the very carefully conducted communal part of the rite and the hastily expedited individual part, and will in consequence only help discredit private confession even more.[6]

In order to avoid this difficulty, care should be taken to have a sufficient number of confessors in attendance to meet the needs of the penitents. Then the personal meeting of penitent and priest will take place in more satisfactory conditions and can be harmoniously integrated into the communal rite which gives it its meaning, at least in part. Pastors should schedule such celebrations at regular intervals throughout the year.

Here, as in the private rite, the confessor must be careful to help the penitent make a truly integral confession, that is, one that does not remain on the surface of things but endeavors to go deeper. Experience shows that participation in a communal rite makes hardly any difference to the confessions of some people; even after the reading of God's word and the examination of conscience they make the same routine accusation as they do, or did, in the private rite. The pastor must make it his aim to help these penitents relate God's word to themselves, revitalize their examination of conscience, and make conversion a fuller reality in their lives.

Once again, all this presupposes that the time needed can be taken. If a pastor cannot gather enough confessors to conduct a careful celebration within a reasonable length of time, he would do better to have recourse to general absolution.

3. General absolution

The new rite contains a ceremony of reconciliation in which general absolution is given. The conditions for the use of this ceremony had already been determined in the Pastoral Norms issued on June 16, 1972.

A response to new needs

In virtue of these Pastoral Norms, general absolution has been authorized in certain dioceses during the final days of Advent and Lent. These celebrations meet a real pastoral need. They bring together a large number of the faithful, so large that the individual confession of each person is not possible in the time available and given the limited number of confessors.

The presence of such crowds is doubtless to be explained by the persisting tradition (still widespread in recent years) that the entire community should come to confession during the final days before the major feasts. Parishes have extended their hours for confession and have urged the faithful to come earlier, but no great change of habits has been effected. On the other hand, the hours during which people work in the cities also create limitations, with the result that most of the confessions must be heard on only a few evenings.

In addition, the number of priests is steadily decreasing, and their average age is increasingly older. Thus it is not as easy as it used to be to find an adequate number of extra confessors to help the parish priests. Moreover, the latter must divide their time between hearing confessions and preparation of the liturgy for the coming feast – this last a work that has become more demanding since the reform of the liturgy.

It is certain that many people who have had recourse to general absolutions would have remained unabsolved for a long time yet and perhaps would have been forever deprived of the grace of the sacrament. Even if it seems at first glance that these individuals could easily find a confessor at another time, the fact is that they do not do so. It can even be said that in practice this is impossible for them for reasons which, as they see them, are cogent: change of mentalities, a negative image of private confession, lack of meaning for them in this rite, and so on. Thanks to communal celebrations and general absolution these people have made their way back to the sacrament of reconciliation. Many individuals showed a surprising interest in the sacrament and a lively desire to celebrate their reconciliation. According to many pastors, these celebrations have been the occasion for individuals to return to the Church after being away from it for a long time. This is evidence of a spiritual need that deserves to be taken seriously and given a positive response by pastors; for some people, general absolution may be the means of their rediscovering the rite of individual reconciliation.

It is rather unfortunate that the Pastoral Norms found their way into the new rite without being modified in the light of experience. In my view, for example, too quantitative an interpretation can falsify the deeper meaning. I am convinced that the conditions required for the imparting of general absolution are verified more often than might seem at first sight to be the case. On the other hand, we should not believe it to be an infallible answer to all the problems of the penitential rite. The Church's experience proves the contrary. In the not too distant future we will have to invent new forms, new rites, because the present ones are no longer suitable.

The conditions required

A priest may grant general sacramental absolution to the faithful who make only a generic confession of their sins "if there is grave need, namely when, in view of the number of penitents, sufficient confessors are not available to hear individual confessions properly within a suitable period of time, so that the penitents would, through no fault of their own, have to go without sacramental grace or holy communion for a long time."[7]

In determining what "a suitable period of time" is, we should not be satisfied with allowing some sacramental minimum. We should rather think in terms of the time required for a suitable celebration as described in the new rite. The reason for holding this kind of a celebration should be a truly pastoral one. This means that the quantitative requirements set by the rite should not be dissociated from properly pastoral concerns, but should rather be judged precisely in this pastoral light.

Here, by way of example, are some truly pastoral objectives that are listed in the Canadian evaluation and report:

– the desire to meet a real spiritual need of the faithful;

– the possibility of contacting a number of non-practicing Catholics who would otherwise not receive the sacrament;

– a pastoral concern to help the participants make serious progress in the process of conversion;

– a desire to follow a common policy with the other parishes and pastors of the region.

Very important is the pedagogical goal of educating the faithful in the meaning of repentance in all its dimensions, personal and ecclesial. If, in an act of radical faith, a number of the faithful gave public expression to their belief that the Church is the community of redeemed human beings who therein manifest their hope, then general absolution would already have its special motivation.

These, then, are the results to be expected from these celebrations. Once again, however, careful preparation must be made. Experience shows that preparation for general absolution must be made weeks in advance, in the form of a preaching of repentance.

The process of conversion is slow and gradual, and can hardly be accomplished fully in a single celebration. In many places a program of coherent catechesis has been implemented throughout Lent, leading to a penance celebration at the end of Lent in preparation for Easter. Others have chosen to develop a kind of penitential process spread over several celebrations. Many other suitable methods can be used. The pastor's creative imagination has plenty of scope here.

What I said earlier applies here as well, and even more so: a celebration of this type cannot be dashed off in fifteen minutes. The proclamation of the word, the examination of conscience, and the prayer need to be done carefully, to say nothing of the act of generic accusation by which sinners signify their intention of conversion and reconciliation.[8]

The proviso of later confession to a priest

When general absolution is given with all desirable care, pastors must themselves be convinced, and must convince their penitents, that there is no reason to doubt the sacramental efficacy of such a rite. The fact that there is a proviso of later confession to a priest does not limit the effectiveness of the absolution received; this in fact reconciles those who receive it in a sincere conversion.

The rite of general absolution contains all that is essential to the sacrament of reconciliation: an act of faith in the salvation won in Jesus Christ, the prayer of the Church, the visible expression of forgiveness. It cannot be emphasized too much that general absolution is preceded by an accusation that is both personal and public. It finds expression, first, in the fact that the sinner attends such a celebration, and, subsequently, in the sign each penitent is invited to make at the moment of absolution in order to show his or her desire for forgiveness.[9]

It is quite understandable that the Pastoral Norms issued in Rome should make it a condition for general absolution that the recipients be required to make a subsequent confession to a priest. Unfortunately, the faithful have not always grasped the real meaning of the proviso. It is quite possible that in regions different from our own the personal confession of all sins to a priest is still the best and surest expression of a genuine conversion. It must also be understood that the conversion that is expressed in this rite of general absolution is only a stage in an ongoing process, that it must be maintained and deepened, and that the individualized rite is the privileged psychological means of doing so. In any event, the personal awareness Christians have of their individual sins and their ways of participating in collective sins will normally impel them to reveal themselves in a formal, explicit self-accusation during a later penitential rite of another type. Consequently, delay in or neglect of the later confession (i.e., accusation) required does not put the penitents back into their earlier state of sin; it may, however, be itself a sin, the seriousness of which depends on the will of the penitent in his or her act of neglect.

This proviso, then, should be presented to the faithful in a positive way, by bringing out the spirit in which it is set down and by showing the intrinsic value of such a detailed accusation. In such an encounter with another Christian the penitent encounters the mediating Church and therein experiences the forgiveness of the Lord. If sinners sincerely want to be reconciled with God and the Church, it is normal that they should be willing to do all that the Church asks when they confess their sins. An unwillingness that expresses a hatred of the law will prevent the effect of the sacrament here and now (i.e., of the general absolution) because this contempt is a sign that the sinner is not truly converted.

Is the delayed accusation to be regarded as an essential condition? I answer without hesitation: No. The situation in which the rite of general absolution places the sinner is different from the situation created when through perfect contrition a sinner regains the state of grace in other circumstances. People are perhaps too much inclined to identify the two situations. In the first case, the absolution given is a genuine sacrament, and a sacrament cannot normally be signified when its essential parts do not coexist. This is why the hypothesis of the anticipated efficacy of the absolution does not apply. In the second case, there is no sacrament. Thus, to assert the likeness of the two situations does not resolve the difficulty.

There are pastors who solve the problem of the deferred accusation by calling its omission a "mortal sin." Are contemporary Christians capable of numerous mortal sins? I would be hesitant in giving an answer to this question. In any case, the distinction between mortal and venial sin would be valid only if the sacrament existed solely in function of mortal sin. As a matter of fact, however, the sacrament is primarily a public affirmation of our faith in the salvation that Jesus Christ has won for us.

Distinction between mortal sin and venial sin

I think I am justified in saying that this distinction is much more juridical than theological or moral. We will look in vain in biblical tradition for the terms "mortal" or "venial," although the reality to which they point is there at bottom. Sins certainly differ in their seriousness, i.e., what we might call their greatness. Jesus tells Pilate that his betrayer is more guilty than Pilate himself: "He who delivered me to you has the greater sin" (Jn 19:11). There are similar texts in both the Old and the New Testaments.

Sins also differ in their effect. We might cite many texts here, the most frequently used being some from St. Paul. In Gal 5:19-21, for instance, Paul lists these "works of the flesh": "immorality, impurity, licentiousness, idolatry, sorcery, enmity, strife, jealousy, anger, selfishness, dissension, party spirit, envy, drunkenness, carousing, and the like." In 1 Cor 6:9-10 he lists the immoral, idolaters, adulterers, homosexuals, thieves, the greedy, drunkards, revilers, and robbers and says that none of these "will inherit the kingdom of God." The sins are therefore "mortal."

Two questions arise: Can we readily identify big sins with mortal sins? What is to be understood by the "kingdom" of which certain sins deprive us?

Many theologians give an affirmative answer to the first question, but an answer that is also so subtle and complicated that St. Augustine's prudent explanation is much more preferable: "God has left this distinction obscure in order to incite us to avoid all sin."[10]

The terms mortal and venial came into Church usage as the result of quite different pastoral concerns. From the texts of St. Paul that I have just cited, it seems quite clear that the early Christian communities were strongly repelled by sin, to the point of first excluding sinners from the community and then restoring them to it. But such a rite of exclusion and reintegration could not be applied to all sins. Understandably, then, St. Paul draws up an initial, very empirical list of sins that are put there not because of their inherent seriousness but rather because of their effect on the community. Being notorious, such sins acted as an invitation to sin for other Christians. The term "kingdom" that St. Paul uses and that brings us to our second question, must be understood as referring to the

Church and not be given the eschatological sense of "heaven."

While not beyond question, this interpretation is surely an acceptable one, especially since Tertullian (as a Montanist) will regard these same sins as unforgivable. It is he who will use the term *mortalia* (mortal) for the first time.[11] We can infer from this that when *The Shepherd of Hermas* allowed a second penance, it was not necessarily instituting a new rite but may simply be recognizing the existing rite as applicable to sins whose special character had formerly caused them to be regarded as unforgivable. In Augustine's time and in subsequent centuries the faithful were presented with lists of sins for which canonical penance had to be done. But what all these have in common is public notoriety. Are we not therefore justified in thinking that in the mind of that day these sins separated men and women from the Church precisely because of their notoriety? They were a sign that Christians living in such a state no longer adhered in a life-giving way to the gospel of Jesus.

In the period of tariff penance, the lists of sins no longer had the same meaning. The lists were correlative with penances to be levied by a priest and not with the penitential rite itself. But when the Fourth Council of the Lateran in 1215 made an annual confession obligatory for those who committed mortal sin, the distinction of mortal and venial acquired a new importance. Once a law is established, there must be a way available of determining who is subject to the law. Since the lists of sins no longer existed, Christians had to be given a means of knowing whether or not they were obliged by the law. Here, I think, we have the key to an understanding of the theological disquisitions of the Scholastics and their successors.

The distinction is important, then, by reason of the law that makes it necessary. For this reason I speak of an "ecclesiastical necessity" and therefore of the distinction as being juridical. Given what I have been saying in this book about the nature and meaning of the sacrament, the distinction has little significance. But it returns to the scene in connection with the proviso necessitating a later detailed accusation of mortal sins. Here again, we are dealing with an ecclesiastical law, and if the law is to be more effective and specific, the institution must tell us what it understands by mortal. The theologians have no firm answer to this juridical question.

In consequence of what I have been saying about the deferred accusation of sins, the ritual must be applied in a pastoral manner. Sinners receiving a general absolution must normally have an at least implicit desire of responding to the call that the Church makes part of the law. And the pastor has no right to remain silent on this point; on the contrary, he must exhort his flock to obey that call. Given the contemporary mentality, it will obviously be necessary to insist on the deferred confession, not because it is the law, but because of the reasons behind the law. The emphasis will be placed more on the *usefulness* and *value* of the confession than on its obligatory character. Certain terms of the proviso are found incomprehensible and unacceptable by many of the faithful; this is a fact that must be taken into account. But this real difficulty in no way detracts from the results we can expect from these celebrations. The important thing is to persevere in the effort to educate the faithful, in reliance on the assistance of the Spirit, so that they may continue on, discover within themselves the values that an individual encounter with the priest embodies, and reach personal conviction on the subject.

4. The nonsacramental celebration of penance

The rite adds a new ritual form for nonsacramental penance celebrations. Especially when these facilitate deeper contact with the word of God, they can be very useful in stimulating and deepening a conversion. This holds for groups of the faithful who wish a fuller preparation for the sacrament; for the new communities that come into existence in various places and that cannot always have a priest present; for schools in their effort to introduce the young to the spirit of reconciliation; and for alienated Christians who, even if they find themselves still far from the sacrament, nonetheless wish to make an effort at reconciliation.

In form these celebrations are quite flexible and are especially suitable for meeting the increasingly varied needs of Christians. It is to be observed that they have a strong resemblance to sacramental celebrations. In my opinion, if these new celebrations multiply, especially because priests are scarce, they will soon make it necessary to look into the possibility of new ministries.[12]

Now that we have reached the end of this discussion of forms, the reader will understand why I chose not to speak of themes that at one time were the subject of lengthy discussion, such as the secret of the confessional, the absolution of an accomplice in sin, or solicitation in the confessional. Once the priest's role is understood in the way I have been endeavoring to explain it, most of the canonical regulations regarding these matters become otiose. It should be remarked, however, that if the institution passed laws in these areas it was certainly not for the pleasure of complicating an already difficult situation but in order to provide remedies for real abuses that had crept in over the years. I dare believe that a serious following of the new rite will not make new, detailed legislation necessary.

I am glad that the new rite takes the form of a simple outline and that those responsible for implementing the rite (episcopal conferences, local Ordinaries, confessors) are able to adapt it.[13] Allow me to hope that there will be some minimum of uniformity so that the faithful of our dioceses will not be thrown off by liturgies that are utterly dissimilar.[14]

I have been presenting the sacrament of reconciliation as an act of faith in a good and merciful God and as an act of reconciliation of Christians among themselves in order that they may then be reconciled with God. The sacrament is a joyous celebration of God's mercy. By way of a conclusion I shall simply suggest meditation on the parable of the Prodigal Son (Lk 15:11-24), for it contains all the elements I have been trying to highlight.

The tragedy of people as sinners — and we are all sinners, like the younger brother in the parable — is that they do not realize or confess their sins unless they are put in an extreme situation. They make us think of the metaphor Hosea uses: "The iniquity of Ephraim is bound up, his sin is kept in store. The pangs of childbirth come for him, but he is an unwise son; for now he does not present himself at the mouth of the womb" (Hos 13:12-13).

Perhaps we are too ready to forget that the main transformation we undergo is interior and that it is the work of the Spirit. The Letter to the Hebrews twice cites the prediction of the prophet Jeremiah as now fulfilled: "The days will come, says the Lord, when I will establish a new covenant with the house of Israel and with the house of Judah; not like the covenant that I made with their fathers on the day when I took them by the hand to lead them out of the land of Egypt; for they did not continue in my covenant, and so I paid no heed to them, says the Lord. This is the covenant that I will make with the house of Israel after those days, says the Lord: I will put my laws into their minds, and write them on their hearts, and I will be their God, and they shall be my people" (Heb 8:8-10; see Jer 31:31-34).

About fifteen years after Jeremiah's prophecy the prophet Ezekiel repeats the prediction but carries it a step further: "And I will give them one heart, and put a new spirit within them; I will take the stony heart out of their flesh and give them a heart of flesh" (Ezek 11:19).

So mighty was the fulfillment of this prophecy that the Holy Spirit is the *New Covenant* and the *New Law*. We enter with will and heart into the New Covenant on condition that we acknowledge and accept the gift of God as the norm of our own life. Only then can we apply to ourselves the joyous message of St. Paul whose baptismal catechesis contains this message: "Sin will have no dominion over you, since you are not under the law but under grace" (Rom 6:14). He shows that this ideal alone effectively closes the door to the arbitrary action of the carnal self; that if human beings accept this ideal with all their hearts, it will preserve them from wickedness.

Strengthened as we are by the joyous hope of salvation in Jesus, we have become more at home with the conception of pastoral care as primarily a service to Jesus Christ and a help to the ecclesial community. In previous generations, the emphasis was rather on the powers of the hierarchy.

In addition, we now understand better that this ministry, even in its liturgical and sacramental form, must be, above all else, a dispensing of the word of God in order to steady Christians in their conversion and strengthen them in their commitment. We understand that believers need to verify the authenticity of the faith they live by. It is the proper task of the Church, the Christian community, to furnish this verification or at least to offer Christians the occasion for it at special seasons of their lives.

The essential function of a pastor is to announce the Good News. When Jesus Christ sent his disciples forth, he expressly told them: "Go therefore and make disciples of all nations, baptizing them in the name of the Father and of the Son and of the Holy Spirit, teaching them to observe all that I have commanded you" (Mt 28:19-20). Doesn't forming consciences mean, above all else, teaching people to follow Jesus who is the Way, the Truth, and the Life?

By proclaiming the life-giving word of God and celebrating the signs of salvation that restore or intensify this life, the pastor makes present the Christ who is God's concrete presence within the human race.

But this presence of God in Christ is a reality in the history of the race only because it acts in a mysterious way in human beings. In a very real manner it sets them on the right path and draws them in their personal history (wherein their personal development in time leads gradually to full self-awareness) toward a revelation of God in this Christ who is with us.

Divine grace, revealed to us in Christ and communicated to us through the ministry of the Church (acting in the priest), is at work in all people, inspiring their quest of the God who has revealed himself. This grace develops in a process marked by a vital continuity, thanks to the dialogue that is initiated on the occasion of the penitential rite and that pastors and faithful engage in on the basis of the life of faith that both parties perceive within the inmost recesses of their being. On the one hand, Christ approaches sinners as one having a human face. On the other, sinners are interiorly drawn toward him.

Experience shows, however, that the life of faith is not something directly evident. It is rare that the signs tradition has made sacred are perfectly attuned, as it were, to the groupings inspired by the mysterious attraction people feel deep inside themselves. Their thinking as believers develops out of an experiential confrontation between divine grace at work in the history of humanity's salvation and divine grace at work in the history of these believers' personal salvation. It is to be expected that this confrontation would give rise to uncertainties, hesitations, and more or less serious shortcomings. Men and women possess themselves fully only in the call to transcendence.

In all Christians there exists a powerful thrust that comes from the divine life in them: from the love of God and the Spirit, from the faith that is an invitation to constant growth. We live today in a society that is being moved by extraordinarily powerful forces and that is growing with great rapidity. If Christian morality continues to appear as a set of prescriptions accompanied by threats and external pressures, it will soon drive Christians to more accessible doctrines and more demanding mysticisms.

Let us rather be drawn by the merciful words of Jesus Christ. Let us be reconciled!

Notes

Notes to Introduction, pp. 1–4

[1] *Constitution on the Sacred Liturgy*, no. 72: AAS 56 (1964) 118; tr. in A. Flannery (ed.), *Vatican II: The Conciliar and Postconciliar Documents* (Collegeville, 1975) 22.

[2] "Committee Report: The Renewal of the Sacrament of Penance," Catholic Theological Society of America, 1975.

[3] *Ibid.*, 34–37.

[4] *Study Text IV: Commentary on the Rite of Penance*, United States Catholic Conference, Washington, D.C., 1975.

[5] Congregation for the Doctrine of the Faith, *Pastoral Norms for General Absolution* (June 16, 1972) in AAS 64 (1972) 510–514, and also *The Pope Speaks* 17 (1972) 280–284 and *Canon Law Digest* 7:667–672. See the comments of Pope Paul VI at his general audience of July 19, 1972, in *The Pope Speaks* 17 (1972) 272–274.

[6] *Ordo Paenitentiae*, promulgated December 2, 1973 (Vatican City, 1974). Translated by the International Commission on English in the Liturgy as *The Rite of Penance* and published in (e.g.) *The Rites of the Catholic Church* (2 vols.; New York, 1976 and 1980) 1:335–445, and *The Rite of Penance* (Collegeville, Minnesota: The Liturgical Press, 1975).

[7] Among general works on the sacrament of penance, these are the ones I consider more important: E. Amann, A. Michel and M. Jugie, "Pénitence," *Dictionnaire de théologie catholique* 12 (1933) 748–1138; M. Mellet and A.-M. Henry, "Penance," in A.-M. Henry (ed.) *Christ in His Sacraments*, tr. by A. Bouchard (Theology Library 6; Chicago, 1958) 203–274; P. Anciaux, *The Sacrament of Penance* (New York: Sheed and Ward, 1962); Carra de Vaux Saint-Cyr, *The Sacrament of Penance* (New York: Paulist Press, 1966); H. Vorgrimler, "Pénitence (sacrement de)," in *Encyclopédie de la foi 2* (Paris, 1966) 411–425 [= translation of "Busssakrament," in *Handbuch theologischer Grundbegriffe* 1 (Munich, 1962) 204–217]; B. Bro, *On demande des pécheurs* (Paris, 1969); B. Häring, *Shalom: Peace, the Sacrament of Reconciliation* (New York: Farrar, Straus & Giroux, 1967); M. J. Taylor (ed.), *The Mystery of Sin and Forgiveness* (Staten Island, N.Y., 1971); Swiss Bishops, "Instruction pastorale sur la pénitence et la confession," *Documentation catholique* 68 (1971) 110–122; Belgian Bishops, "Instruction pastorale sur la pénitence," *Documentation catholique* 70 (1973) 913–918, 975–979, 1028–1033; P. Tripier, *La réconciliation. Un sacrement pour l'espérance* (Paris, 1976); F. Sottocornola, "Penitenza (sacramento della)," in *Dizionario Teologico Interdisciplinare* (Turin, 1977) 690–706.

To the above list the following works are added: W. J. Bausch, *It is the Lord! Sin and Penance Revisited* (Notre Dame: Ave Maria Press, 1970); F. J. Buckley, *"I Confess." The Sacrament of Penance Today* (Notre Dame: Ave Maria Press, 1972); J. D. Crichton, *The Ministry of Reconciliation* (London: Geoffrey Chapman, 1974); W. Freburger, *Repent and Believe. The Celebration of the Sacrament of Penance* (Notre Dame: Ave Maria Press, 1971); T. Guzie, *What a Modern Catholic Believes About Confession* (Chicago: Thomas More Press, 1974); L. Orsy, *The Evolving Church and the Sacrament of Penance* (Denville, New Jersey, 1978); K. Rahner, *Allow Yourself to Be Forgiven: Penance Today* (Denville, New Jersey, 1974).

95

For an extensive bibliography of some 562 entries, see "Bibliography on Penance (1965–1972)" in "Committee Report: The Renewal of the Sacrament of Penance," The Catholic Theological Society of America (1975) 49–95.

Notes to Chapter 1, pp. 7–14

[1] I have used the data for Canada in particular.

[2] *Rapport préliminaire,* 4; see *Rapport final du Comité d'étude de la C.C.C.,* (April, 1971) 2–9.

[3] Writing in a humorous vein, Msgr. Raymond Lavoie puts penitents into five categories:

"There are the good-living aristocrats who commit no sins or at least commit only unconscious sins. They have a confessor . . . who discourses sublimely to them at each confession, as the Church's tribute to their status as distinguished practicing Catholics. . . .

"There is also the countless throng of men and women . . . who see you [confessors] first and foremost as judges who possess the power of the keys and will open the gates of Paradise only to those they arbitrarily predestine for this lot. . . . These people confess directly to God because it's a less complicated process. . . .

"A certain number of Christians have kept the habit of monthly or almost monthly confession. They are all people of fifty or over; one-third of them are men, two-thirds women. . . . They look for indulgences, being deeply moved with pity over the destiny of their deceased and knowing that this precious commodity is to be acquired only at the price of monthly confession. . . .

"Another category of penitents, which has now disappeared for the greater glory of God, is made up of those faithful whom our cousins in France call 'Easter people' (*pascalisants*). . . . These believers were often profoundly lacking in proper dispositions and were the plague of our confessionals, because of their quality and their numbers, during the exhausting sessions we had to face during Holy Week. . . . For all our absolutions were they in fact forgiven? . . .

"Finally, there are the generous, loving, faithful, fervent Christians who are grappling with the difficulties of birth regulation and waiting for menopause. They try to make their children understand the importance of frequent communion. They love to attend Sunday Mass with their families. It is such a normal thing for people to eat together when they truly love one another! But the combination of thermometer and calendar is not always an effective safeguard, and the family doctor can find no medical reason for prescribing the pill. In such circumstances slips tend to become chronic. . . . We taught them that when the Eucharist is received with love, it purifies their souls of all the shadows left by these little deviations. Never could they have believed that good parents could be barred from communion. And yet, despite all their contrition, they are so barred." In: R. Lavoie and P. Ouellet, *Monsieur le curé et Monsieur le vicaire ont-ils le vrai visage du Christ?* (Quebec, 1972) 5–8.

[4] Social pressure is another important factor in society that we would be wrong to neglect. There was a time when it really would have been an act of daring not to go to confession at certain times of the liturgical year. Mother, father, and children all went to confession at Christmas; on this occasion even the notables of the parish were spurred to action, since they would not risk giving a bad example to hardened sinners.

"Everybody does it; go along with the crowd," says public opinion even today. Unfortunately, the slogan is also reversed today: No one else does it; why should I? No one else goes to confession; why should I? Very few are strong enough to resist this sociopsychological pressure because – this is at least a partial reason – they have no motives urging them to resist adopting the kind of behavior that is popular. Their understanding of the sacrament of penance is too vague to condition the way Christians act.

⁵ It is clear that the kind of thinking I have been explaining has already affected pastoral practice in some places:

"The aim of pastoral care is to restore to present-day Christians the meaning of sin, conversion and reconciliation, while taking into account the new emphases characteristic of the modern conscience: awareness of shared responsibility, a sense of duty toward society, concern for acting in a personal and lucid manner before God. This education in moral responsibility and in the sense of sin must be the basis for any step taken in the matter of penance.

"The reason why Christians fail to recognize their sinfulness and no longer have (as people say) any sense of sin is that they no longer realize the depth of God's love for them; they are no longer overwhelmed by the revelation of the Father's love and by the redemption Jesus Christ has accomplished. The real impulse to repentance comes from the consciousness of being unfaithful to love of God in the course of life" (*Directives pastorales de Saint-Jérôme* [1972] 1–2).

⁶ For further study see W. J. Burghardt, *Towards Reconciliation* (Washington: U.S. Catholic Conference, 1974); B. J. Cooke, "The Social Aspects of the Sacrament of Penance," in *Proceedings of the Catholic Theological Society of America* 22 (1967) 173–183; J. Jossua, "Crise et redécouverte du sacrement de pénitence," *Revue des sciences philosophiques et théologiques* 52 (1967) 119–142; E. Kennedy, *A Sense of Life, A Sense of Sin. Personal Morality Today*, Garden City, N.Y., 1975; K. Menninger, *Whatever Became of Sin?* (New York: Hawthorn Books, Inc., 1973); L. Robitaille, "Le sacrement de la pénitence: Etat de la question et prospectives," *Liturgie et vie chrétienne*, no. 71 (1970) 5–13; J. Shea, *What a Modern Catholic Believes About Sin*, Chicago, 1971.

Notes to Chapter 2, pp. 15–31

¹ I wrote this chapter with the collaboration of a colleague, Rev. Jean-Louis D'Aragon, S.J., professor in the Faculty of Theology at the University of Montreal. I thank him for the light he has shed on the subject.

² G. von Rad, *Old Testament Theology*, tr. by D. M. G. Stalker, 1 (New York, 1962) 369–370, 395ff.

³ See *Rule* (1 QS), 1:23 – 2:1.

⁴ Cited in H. Strack and P. Billerbeck, *Kommentar zum Neuen Testament aus Talmud und Midrasch* 1:170.

⁵ *Exhomologesis*: Tertullian will use the word to designate the penitential rite. See his *De paenitentia* VII, IX and X. "This action, usually given a Greek name, is *exhomologesis*, in which we confess our sins to the Lord . . . because confession paves the way for satisfaction, repentance is born of confession, and God's anger is allayed by repentance" (IX,2; CCL 1:336).

⁶ See 1 QS 6,24 – 7,25.

⁷ For this, the reader may profitably refer to P. Bonnard, *L'Evangile selon saint Matthieu* (Paris – Neuchâtel, 1970) 244–246, 274–276, or P. F. Ellis, *Matthew: His Mind and His Message* (Collegeville, 1974) 67–72.

⁸ "My view is that these verses are an instruction regarding disciplinary practice in the Syro-Palestinian Christian churches of the eighties; the instruction is based on the teaching of Jesus and his behavior in dealing with the little ones" (Bonnard, *op. cit.,* 273–274).

⁹ *Rite of Penance,* no. 2; see Council of Trent, session 14, canon 10 (DS 1710).

¹⁰ See Council of Trent, session 14, chapter 6 (DS 1684).

¹¹ In chapter 5 I shall discuss the theological interpretation of "binding and loosing."

¹² See Jas 5:16-20: "Therefore confess your sins to one another, and pray for one another, that you may be healed . . ."

¹³ See Vorgrimler, art. cit., 416–417.

¹⁴ To supplement what has been said in this chapter, the reader may consult, in addition to works already cited, the following: E. Cooper, "Understanding Sin in the New Testament," *Louvain Studies* 1 (1967) 298–311; J. F. Craghan, "The Bible and Reconciliation," *American Ecclesiastical Review* 169 (1975) 164–190; A. Dirksen, *The New Testament Concept of Metanoia,* Washington, D.C., 1932; J. Giblet and P. Grelot, "Repentance/Conversion," in X. Leon-Dufour (ed.), *Dictionary of Biblical Theology,* tr. by P. J. Cahill and E. M. Stewart (2nd ed.; New York, 1973) 486–491; E. Lepinski, *La liturgie pénitentielle dans la Bible* (Lectio divina 52; Paris, 1969); S. Lyonnet and L. Sabourin, *Sin, Redemption and Sacrifice. A Biblical and Patristic Study,* Analecta Biblica 48, Rome, 1970; J. Murphy-O'Connor, "Péché et communauté dans le Nouveau Testament," *Revue biblique* 74 (1967) 161–193; R. Schnackenburg, *The Moral Teaching of the New Testament,* Freiburg, 1965; *Sin, Salvation, and the Spirit,* ed. D. Durken, Collegeville, Minnesota, 1979; C. Stuhlmueller, *Reconciliation: A Biblical Call,* Chicago, 1975; H. Vorgrimler, "Matthieu 16, 18s, et le sacrement de pénitence," in *L'homme devant Dieu: Mélanges Henri de Lubac* (Theologie 56; Lyons, 1963) 1:51-61.

Notes to Chapter 3, pp. 32–45

¹ Clement of Rome, *Epistola ad Corinthios* 8, 1. 2. 5: "The ministers of God's grace, under the inspiration of the Holy Spirit, have spoken of repentance, and the Master of the universe himself has spoken of repentance and sworn an oath: As I live, says the Lord, I do not desire the sinner's death so much as his conversion (Ezek 33:11). . . . In his desire that all whom he loves should repent, this is what the all-powerful will of God has decided."

² *Epistola duodecim apostolorum* 47–48. See C. Vogel, *Le pécheur et la pénitence dans l'Eglise ancienne* (Chrétiens de tous les temps 15; Paris, 1966) 62.

³ See *Pastor Hermae* IV, 3: "'But for those who were called before these last days the Lord has prescribed repentance. For the Lord, who knows hearts and is aware of all things beforehand, foresaw the weakness of human beings and the great wickedness of the demon; he foresaw that the demon would inflict evil on the servants of God and would be set against them. In his great mercy the Lord has taken pity on his creatures and instituted this repentance, and he has given me authority over the repentance. I say to you,' he said, 'if after this serious and solemn call anyone tempted by the demon falls into sin, he can do penance once. But if he sins again and repents, his repentance will be useless to him.'" For the entire text see H. Karpp, *La pénitence: Textes et commentaires des origines de l'ordre pénitentiel de l'Eglise an-*

cienne (Neuchâtel, 1970) 57; also available in *The Faith of the Early Fathers,* selected and tr. by W. A. Jurgens (Collegeville, 1970) 1:32-37.

⁴ The controversy is described in B. Poschmann, *Penance and the Anointing of the Sick,* New York: 1964, 38–62.

⁵ The Montanist movement seems to have been essentially a reaction against excessive mildness in dealing with sinners. An oracle of the Paraclete, given through the mouth of Montanus, sums up perfectly the attitude of the Phrygian mystics: "The Church can forgive sins, but I will not forgive them lest others then sin" (Tertullian, *De pudicitia* XXI, 7; CCL 2:1326). According to this statement the forgiveness of postbaptismal sins is possible but the Church should not grant it lest her action strike the faithful as an invitation to sin. Tertullian, the theoretician of the movement, rejects the principles he had accepted in his *De paenitentia* (VII; IX; X) and challenges the Church's right to forgive all sins; he distinguishes between forgivable sins and the unforgivable sins which he calls *mortalia* ("deadly"). Here for the first time in the Church we hear the expression "mortal sins." We should note that in Tertullian it refers to sins for which the Church must refuse forgiveness; in order to determine just which sins these are, the Church should look to Paul's trilogy of sins, of which adultery is one. The treatise on chastity (*De pudicitia*) is of great interest here. (See Karpp, *op. cit.,* 183–225; Jurgens, *op. cit.,* 159–160.)

⁶ See *De paenitentia* IX: "[Confession] commands one to lie in sackcloth and ashes, to cover the body with mourning, to cast the spirit down in sorrow, to exchange the sins which have been committed for a demeanor of sorrow; to take no other food or drink except what is plain, not, of course, for the sake of the stomach, but for the sake of the soul; and most of all, to feed prayers on fasting; to groan, to weep and wail day and night to the Lord your God; to bow before the presbyters, to kneel before God's refuge places, and to beseech all the brethren for the embassy of their own supplication" (Jurgens, *op. cit.,* 131).

⁷ See *Sermones* 351 and 352 (PL 39).

⁸ As in Augustine, *Sermo* 232, 8: "Some sinners have freely entered the ranks of the penitents; others have been excommunicated by us and forced to enter those ranks" (PL 38:1111).

⁹ If only such sins as were public knowledge were subject to canonical penance, Augustine's words are easy to interpret: "Penitents are numerous here; when hands are being laid on them, a long line forms. . . . I examine them and I find some to be of evil life. . . . The place that should be a place of self-humbling becomes a place of sin instead. I address you, you who call yourselves penitents but are not; I address you, but what am I to say to you? Shall I address words of praise to you? Certainly not! I weep and am sorrowful, but how else am I to act? Change your lives, change your lives, I beg you! . . . Let us admit that life is long; I seek even a single penitent, but I find none" (*Sermo* 232, 8–9; PL 38:1111–12).

¹⁰ *Epistola* 168 (to the bishops of Campania, Samnium and Picenum), no. 2: "I have recently learned that a manner of acting contrary to apostolic rule has been illegally introduced, and I now order its suppression. In connection with the penance required of the faithful no written list of sins in detail is to be read publicly . . ." (PL 54:1210–11).

¹¹ Note the text cited above in n. 9. The Council of Agde (506) is also quite explicit in its fifteenth canon: "When penitents ask to do penance, the bishop receives them through a laying on of hands and gives them a hairshirt; if they do not shave their heads and change their garments, they are to be excluded   " (CCl 148:201).

[12] See St. Caesarius of Arles, *Sermones* 67, 179, 189, and 197. There is a French translation in Vogel, *op. cit.,* 155–165.

[13] The penances most often mentioned are fasting, almsgiving, the wearing of a hairshirt, the wearing of dark-colored garments, the shaving of the head, the neglect of cleanliness. People thought it unconceivable that a person should be exteriorly clean while being interiorly corrupt. (See the texts just cited; also the Council of Elvira in 306 and the Council of Sardica in 343.)

[14] "May the passion of our Lord Jesus Christ, the merits of the Blessed Virgin Mary and all the saints, whatever good you do or evil you endure, bring you the forgiveness of your sins, the increase of grace, and the reward of everlasting life. Amen."

[15] Tertullian, *De paenitentia* X, 6: "Wherever one or two of the faithful are, there the Church is, but the Church is Christ. Therefore, when you stretch out your hands toward the knees of your brethren it is Christ whom you touch, it is Christ with whom you plead; when the brethren in turn shed tears over you, it is Christ who suffers, it is Christ who pleads with his Father. What a child asks for is quickly given" (CCL 1:337).

[16] [The phrase *non bis in eodem* means "no double punishment for the same sin," i.e., monks and priests were reduced to the lay state but were not excommunicated as well. — Tr.]

[17] See the Council of Agde (506), canon 15: "Only with reluctance may penance be granted to those still young, because they are at a weak age" (CCL 148:201); Council of Orleans (538), canon 27: "Let no one presume to grant penance to those who are still young. Let no one presume to grant it to married persons without the consent of the other partner and unless the spouses are already advanced in years" (CCL 148A:124).

[18] *De paenitentia* X, 1: "In my view, the majority of Christians shirk repentance or postpone it from day to day because they are afraid to step forward publicly, being more careful of their self-esteem than they are of their salvation. They are like people who have contracted a disease in the private parts of their body and hide it from the doctors; they and their modesty perish together" (CCL 1:337).

[19] Canon 13: "With regard to the dying, the ancient canonical rule is to be observed: no one who is dying is to be deprived of the final, indispensable viaticum" (DS 129).

[20] Canon 18: "Laypersons who do not receive communion on Christmas, Easter, and Pentecost are no longer considered to be Catholics and have no longer a place among them" (CCL 148:202).

[21] *Sermo* 82, 8, 11 (PL 38:511).

[22] *De diversis quaestionibus LXXXIII,* q. 26 (PL 40:18).

[23] Vogel, *op. cit.,* 48–49; see also his essay, "Sin and Penance," in P. Delhaye et al., *Pastoral Treatment of Sin,* tr. by C. Schaldenbrand, F. O'Sullivan and E. Demarchelier (New York, 1968) 258–259.

[24] Council of Châlon-sur-Saône (813), canon 33: "Some say we must confess our sins to God alone; others, that we must confess them to a priest. Both practices are current in the Church and both are the source of great benefit. We are therefore to confess our sins to God alone — God who alone forgives them — and we are to say with David: 'I have made my sin known to you; I have not hidden my wickedness'" (MGH ConcAK I/1:280).

[25] See the commentary of C. Vogel in his *Le pécheur et la pénitence au Moyen-Age* (Chrétiens de tous les temps 30; Paris, 1969) 202–203.

[26] St. Caesarius says that there are three ways of obtaining penance on one's deathbed:

—*a detestable manner:* that of sinners who in their lifetime have never given a thought to conversion but call for the priest at the moment of death. The effects of a reconciliation granted under these conditions are more than doubtful;

—*a good manner:* that of those faithful who have sinned more through weakness than through wickedness and who pass through a sincere conversion when they reach their final hour;

—*a recommended manner:* this consists in preparing oneself throughout one's life for the final reconciliation, the only one given, by a profoundly Christian life, by prayer, fasting, and mortification. Believers who act thus can be assured of God's forgiveness even if they die without being reconciled. If they also have the penitential rite, it will bring them increased grace. (St. Caesarius of Arles, *Sermo* 60; text in Vogel, *Le pécheur . . . dans l'Eglise ancienne,* 149–152.)

This period began the custom of bestowing the anointing of the sick on the dying, as a substitute for the penitential rite in the case of those who could not do the mortifications that the penitential rite involved. The anointing of the sick thus became a penitential rite and would be called "Last Anointing" (Extreme Unction). We may recall the words that until recently accompanied the rite of anointing: "Through this holy anointing and his loving mercy may the Lord forgive you any sins you have committed by the sense of. . . ."

[27] For a complete study of the penitentials see G. Le Bras, "Pénitentiels," *Dictionnaire de théologie catholique* 12:1160–79; and J. McNeill and H. Gamer, *Medieval Handbooks of Penance, A Translation of the Principal libri poenitentiales and Selections from Related Documents,* New York, 1938.

[28] See Vogel, *Le pécheur . . . au Moyen-Age,* 191–192.

[29] Vogel, *ibid.,* 192.

[30] *Capitulare ecclesiasticum* (810–813), c. 15: "Each priest is to have a catalogue listing serious and less serious sins, so that he may be able to defend himself against the snares of the demon and teach the faithful to do the same for themselves" (MGH Cap. Reg. Franc. 1:179). There are many other texts in Vogel, *ibid.,* 194–196.

[31] See, e.g., St. Gregory the Great, *Homilia 26 in evangelia* 6: "You must scrutinize the sin and the penance that followed upon it, and absolve those to whom almighty God has already given the grace of repentance. For the absolution will be effective only if it is in accord with the decision of the interior judge. . . . We must use our pastoral authority to absolve those whom we know to be already living the life of grace. . . . Pastors must weigh carefully their decisions to bind and loose. . . . A pastor must be careful not to bind and loose in an undiscerning manner. Believers who are under the pastor's authority will be fearful about being bound even unjustly, but they are not to rebel rashly against even an unjust sentence" (PL 76:1200–1). The inspiration behind this passage is clearly St. Paul's warning to Timothy: "Do not be hasty in the laying on of hands" (1 Tim 5:20). We also get a glimpse here of the *ex opere operato* of later centuries as the juridical form the sacrament of penance will take.

[32] Council of Tours, canon 22 (MGH ConcAK I/1:789).

[33] Canon 38: "The books called 'penitentials' are to be rejected and eliminated without regret; they are filled with obvious errors and are by unreliable authors" (MGH ConcAK I/1:280).

[34] Council of Paris, chapter 82: "Many priests, out of negligence or ignorance, impose penances on their penitents in a different manner than the canons provide. To this end they use noncanonical booklets called 'penitentials' . . . We all deem it necessary that each bishop in his diocese should have these unauthentic booklets hunted out and burned, in order to prevent ignorant priests from leading their faithful astray in the future" (MGH ConcAK I/2:633).

[35] Alain of Lille, *Regulae de sacra theologia* 85 (PL 210:665).

[36] Fourth Lateran Council (1215), canon 21: "All the faithful of either sex, once they have reached the age of discretion, must confess their sins to their priest at least once a year, perform the penance given them to the best of their ability, and devoutly receive the sacrament of the Eucharist at least at Easter. . . . If they do not obey this rule they are excluded from the Church during life and may not receive Christian burial when they die" (DS 812).

[37] For further details see L. Hamelin, "L'aveu dans la pénitence sacramentelle," *Prêtre et pasteur,* no. 76 (1973) 57–65.

[38] In order to flesh out this historical sketch, the reader may consult the authors already mentioned as well as the following: M.-F. Berrouard, "La pénitence publique durant les six premiers siècles," *Maison-Dieu* 118 (1974) 92–130; J. Bossy, "The Social History of Confession in the Age of the Reformation," *Transactions of the Royal Historical Society,* 5 ser., 25 (1975) 21–38; E. Bourque, *Histoire de la pénitence-sacrement,* Bibliotheque théologique de Laval 11; Quebec, 1947; M.-B. Carra de Vaux Saint-Cyr, "The Sacrament of Penance: An Historical Outline," in *The Mystery of Sin and Forgiveness,* ed. M. Taylor, Staten Island, N.Y., 1971; F. Courtney, "The Administration of Penance I: Ancient Public Penance," *Clergy Review* 46 (1961) 10–27; F. Courtney, "The Administration of Penance II: The Development of Private Penance," *Clergy Review* 46 (1961) 85–98; J. Dallen, "The Imposition of Hands in Penance: A Study in Liturgical History," *Worship* 51 (1977) 224–247; H. Dörries, "The Place of Confession in Ancient Monasticism," *Studia Patristica* 5, *Texte und Untersuchungen,* Band 80, Berlin, 1962, 284–308; P. Galtier, *Aux origines du Sacrement de Pénitence,* Analecta Gregoriana 54, Rome, 1951; M. Mellet, "History of the Sacrament of Penance," in A.-M. Henry et al, *Christ in His Sacraments,* tr. by A. Bouchard (Theology Library 6: Chicago, 1958) 205–222; G. Mitchell, "The Origins of Irish Penance," *Irish Theological Quarterly* 22 (1955) 1–14; R. C. Mortimer, *The Origins of Private Penance in the Western Church,* Oxford, 1939; P. Riga, *Penance in Ambrose, Leo and in the Sermons of Reconciliation of the Roman Archdeacon,* Doctoral dissertation, Graduate Theological Union, Berkeley, California, 1974 (University Microfilms International. Order: HFF 74-23710); J. A. Spitzig, *Sacramental Penance in the 12th and 13th Century,* Studies in Sacred Theology, ser. 2, vol. 6, Washington, D.C., 1947; T. N. Tengler, *Sin and Confession on the Eve of the Reformation,* Princeton, N.J., 1977; O. D. Watkins, *A History of Penance, Being a Study of the Authorities,* vol. I: *The Whole Church to A.D. 450;* vol. II: *The Western Church from A.D. 450 to A.D. 1215;* London, 1920, reprinted New York, 1961.

Notes to Chapter 4, pp. 49–63

[1] See K. Menninger, *Whatever Became of Sin?,* New York, Hawthorn Books, Inc., 1973, 13–37.

[2] *Rite of Penance,* no. 6a, *op. cit.*

[3] I am reminded here of this fine passage of Rahner: "Consider, in the light of the simplest principles of the faith, what must already have happened before confession and absolution! There has been a miracle of grace. For only in that way does a man come to that repentance without which the sacrament would be a sacrilege. There is no contrition of any significance for salvation unless God's gratuitous grace has already anticipated man *so that* he may be able to repent and actually does repent, since the capacity and the actual doing are God's grace. But this miracle of grace does not simply fall from heaven. It too has an incarnational nature: it is a miracle of the grace *of Christ*. It is conditioned by the historical event of Christ and of his Cross, by the preaching of the Word of God in the Church; it may depend on the example and word of another Christian which in the last analysis does also originate in the grace of God; it is given as a gift to man, because and in so far as he is baptized and a member of the Church. Even before the *Ego te absolvo* there has already taken place a miracle of grace in the *Church*. And this miracle is also sustained by the intercessory prayer of the Church" (Karl Rahner, "Forgotten Truths Concerning the Sacrament of Penance," in his *Theological Investigations* 2, tr. by K.-H. Kruger [Baltimore, 1963] 164).

[4] See, e.g., W. Bekkers, "Mercy and the Sacrament of Penance," in *God's People on the March*, New York, 1966, 33–48; D. R. Belgum, *Guilt: Where Religion and Psychology Meet*, Englewood Cliffs, N.J., 1963; E. Berggren, *The Psychology of Confession*, Leiden, 1975; E. J. Farrell, "Penance: Return of the Heart," *Review for Religious* 29 (1970) 677–686; J. Fillela, "Confession as a Means of Self-Improvement," in *The Mystery of Sin and Forgiveness, op. cit.*, 181–202; B. Häring, *Confession and Happiness*, Derby, N.Y., 1966; D. M. Knight, *Confession Can Change Your Life*, Chicago, 1977; G. S. Sloyan, *How Do I Know I'm Doing Right? Toward the Formation of Christian Conscience*, Dayton, Ohio, 1971.

[5] See *Rite of Penance*, no. 6b.

[6] Council of Trent, Session XIV, chapter 5, canons 6 and 7: "If any one denies that sacramental confession has been established by divine law or that it is necessary for salvation in virtue of that same law . . . let him be anathema"; "If any one says that, in order to obtain the forgiveness of sins in the sacrament of penance, it is not necessary by divine law to confess each and every mortal sin one recalls through due and careful examination . . . let him be anathema" (DS 1706–7).

[7] DS 1679.

[8] See *Rite of Penance*, no. 6b: "This inner examination of heart and the exterior accusation should be made in the light of God's mercy."

[9] See J. Ramos-Regidor, "'Reconciliation' in the Primitive Church and Its Lessons for Theology and Pastoral Practice Today," in E. Schillebeeckx (ed.), *Sacramental Reconciliation* (Concilium 61; New York, 1971) 85. "It would be a mistake to assume that the essence of this sacrament consists in accusing oneself of one's sins." After an examination of conscience has been made, it is not *one's sins* (the calculation of which is bound to be erroneous) but *oneself, the sinner*, that goes to meet the Lord. Note also L. Hamelin, *op. cit.*

[10] See *Tractatus in evangelium Joannis* 124, 5: "God does not always remit all the temporal punishments due to sin at the same time as he remits the eternal guilt and punishment. . . . The punishment lasts longer than the sin, lest the sin seem to have been a small thing if the punishment for it ended when the sin itself was forgiven" (CCL 36:683–84). This point is so self-evident for Augustine that he does not hesitate

to say: "If sin did not have to be punished it would not be sin" (*Enarrationes in Psalmos* 44, 18 [PL 36:504]). He even exhorts the sinner: "Love his mercy but at the same time love his truthfulness, for mercy cannot eliminate his justice, nor his justice his mercy. What does he hate? Wickedness. Therefore do you hate it as well, so that you may both hate the same thing. . . . Sin is your doing; set about punishing your sins, for punished they must be, either by you or by him" (*Sermo* 20, 2 [PL 38:138–39]).

[11] It would be of interest here to see how the theology of indulgences developed in terms of expiation for the punishments due to sins. On this subject see Poschmann, *op. cit.*, 210–232 and K. Rahner, "Remarks on the Theology of Indulgences," in his *Theological Investigations* 2:175–201. See also the Apostolic Constitutions of Paul VI: *Paenitemini* (February 17, 1966), and *Indulgentiarum doctrina* (January 1, 1967).

[12] Council of Trent, Session XIV, chapter 8: "They [priests] should bear in mind that the satisfaction they impose is intended not only to safeguard the new life and heal weakness but also to avenge and punish past sins" (DS 1692).

[13] No. 6c. See L. Hamelin, "Aveu et satisfaction," *Liturgie et vie chrétienne,* no. 71 (1970) 38–47.

[14] Here are some suggested books and articles that will supplement my remarks on sin and conversion: H. Allard, "New Views on Mortal Sin," *Clergy Review* 57 (1972) 468–471; G. C. Berkouwer, *Sin,* Grand Rapids, Michigan, 1971; A. Cody, "Sin and Its Sequel in the Story of David and Bathsheba," in *Sin, Salvation, and the Spirit,* Collegeville, 1979, 115–126; E. J. Cooper, "A Newer Look at the Theology of Sin," *Louvain Studies* 3 (1971) 259–307; A. Dirksen, "Metanoeite: The Scriptural Idea of Repentance and Conversion," *The Bible Today* 19 (1965) 1261–1269; A. Dirksen, *The New Testament Concept of Metanoia,* Washington, D.C., 1932; J. Giblet, "God's Fidelity: Men's Sin; Conversion; Retribution," *The God of Israel, The God of Christians,* New York, 1961, 149–196; C. Honders, "Let Us Confess Our Sins. . . ,: in H. Schmidt and D. Power (eds.), *Liturgical Experience of Faith,* Concilium 82, New York, 1973, 86–94; J. B. Metz (ed.), *Moral Evil under Challenge,* Concilium 56, New York, 1970; L. Monden, *Sin, Liberty and Law,* tr. by Donceel, New York, 1965; P. Ricoeur, *The Symbolism of Evil,* tr. by E. Buchanan, New York, 1967.

Notes to Chapter 5, pp. 64–74

[1] *Sermo* 352, 3–8. The metaphor of Lazarus being raised from the dead is used a number of times: see *Sermo* 98, 6; *Tractatus in Evangelium Joannis* 121, 4. St. Gregory the Great uses it later on: *Homilia 26 in Evangelia* 6. Worth reading is F. Van der Meer, *Augustine the Bishop,* tr. by B. Battershaw and G. R. Lamb (New York, 1961; Harper Torchbook ed., 1965) 382–387.

[2] Readers wishing information can consult Poschmann, *op. cit.,* 155–93, or Anciaux, *op. cit.*

[3] See Council of Trent, session XIV, chapter 6 (DS 1684–85).

[4] Since the 1920's theologians have taken this different view, the impulse to it coming from Xiberta's dissertation of 1922. C. Dumont, "La réconciliation en Eglise et la nécessité de l'aveu sacramentel," *Nouvelle revue théologique* 81 (1959), 578–587, sums up this understanding in three propositions:

"Reconciliation with the Church is the direct and specific result of sacramental absolution and, at the same time, an efficacious sign of God's forgiveness.

"This first statement must be understood within a broader vision both of the Church and of the idea of sacrament; the central characteristic of this vision is that the Church is seen as prolonging the visibility of Christ who is the primordial sacrament.

"This conception is fully in accord with the spirit of primitive tradition and is clearly consonant with the entire outlook of scripture that consistently describes union with God as attained in an encounter with the chosen people in the Church of Christ."

K. Rahner finds in Scripture the key to a different understanding: "'Binding' and 'loosing' are not two sides of an alternative, but two phases of the one reaction whereby the Holy Church answers the sin of one of her members. At least this is so in the intention of the Church. When she binds, she binds in order to be able to loose. Only once the truth, which is covered up by the outward appearances of belonging to the Church, has been brought to light on the visible plane of the Church, can the guilt towards the Church and God be lifted or 'loosed' again on the same plane, i.e., on the sacramental plane" ("Forgotten Truths Concerning the Sacrament of Penance," *op. cit.,* 142–143).

⁵ As maintained, e.g., by P. Galtier, *De paenitentia* (Rome, 1950) 125, 171. This is how the Council of Trent understood it, while adding the power to impose a satisfaction.

⁶ In its note explaining the passage in Matthew the French *Ecumenical Translation of the Bible* maintains Bonnard's explanation: "The verbs *bind* and *loose* are not to be interpreted any differently; in contemporary Judaism they meant to *prohibit* and *allow* and, in the last analysis, to *exclude from* and *bring back into* the religious community" (p. 89, note f; see Bonnard, *op. cit.,* 246).

⁷ See E. Schillebeeckx, *Christ the Sacrament of the Encounter with God,* tr. by P. Barrett, et al. (New York, 1963).

⁸ The reader will recognize here a favorite theme of St. John: "The Son can do nothing of his own accord, but only what he sees the Father doing; for whatever he does, that the Son does likewise" (5:19); "I have come down from heaven, not to do my own will, but the will of him who sent me" (6:38); "My teaching is not mine, but his who sent me" (7:16); ". . . I do nothing on my own authority but speak thus as the Father taught me" (8:28); "I speak of what I have seen with my Father . . ." (8:38).

⁹ Poschmann, *op. cit.,* 103.

¹⁰ I have done some research on this problem for the study commission of the Canadian Catholic Conference. I give here the results of my investigations.

¹¹ Cited by Vogel, *Le pécheur . . . au Moyen-Age,* 202–203.

¹² See my essay, "Péché et conversion. Le rite pénitentiel, moyen de réconciliation dans l'Eglise," in *San Bonaventura, maestro di Vita Francescana e di Sapienza Cristiana* (Acts of the International Congress, 1974; Rome, 1976), 404–406: "In reading this text it is difficult to understand how De Vaux Saint-Cyr can say: 'But before continuing this quick survey of the history of doctrines, we may ask what basis there is for this attractive hypothesis [of the two ways]? The answer is simple: there is *no basis.* No one has ever offered anything resembling a proof. The idea has caught on . . . because it gives a simple and clear explanation of the necessity of confession. But there is absolutely nothing, either in the Fathers or in the great twelfth- and thirteenth-century theologians, to justify the notion of two possible ways of obtaining forgiveness.'" For some references see Poschmann, *op. cit.,* 166–167.

¹³ By way of confirmation I may quote here the words of the Belgian bishops: "Reconciliation with the Church plays an essential mediational role in the forgiveness of sins: the sacrament of penance first restores sinners to ecclesiastical communion

(*res et sacramentum*) and thereby to communion with God as well (*res sacramenti*). From this point of view, communal celebrations of penance are more in keeping with authentic tradition and with Scripture, even if their success is not due solely to the emphasis on our solidarity in sin as well as in forgiveness. . . . Since Vatican II a favorite theme has been that the entire Church, the body made up of pastors and faithful, is the visible sacrament of salvation, and there has been an emphasis on the common priesthood of all believers (*Constitution on the Church*). In this perspective, and in keeping with one interpretation of the scriptural texts, some do not hesitate to teach that the entire Church is likewise responsible for the *service* of reconciliation" (*op. cit.*, p. 17).

[14] R. Didier, *La pénitence, sacrement de la réconciliation de l'humanité en Jésus-Christ* (course given at the Theological Faculty of Lyons; Lyons, 1965).

[15] In the next chapter I shall come back to the distinction between mortal and venial sin.

[16] The explanation I give here differs from that of Karl Rahner in his article, "Forgotten Truths Concerning the Sacrament of Penance," 149–152. See also K. Rahner, "The Meaning of Frequent Confession of Devotion," in his *Theological Investigations* 3, tr. by K.-H. and B. Kruger (Baltimore, 1967) 177–189; A.-M. Roguet, "La confession des péchés veniels," *Maison-Dieu*, no. 96 (1967) 209–222; S. M. Ferigle, "Frequent Confession," *Homiletic and Pastoral Review* 76 (1975) 15–24; B. Kelly, "The Confession of Devotion," *Irish Theological Quarterly* 33 (1966) 84–91; J. J. Killgallon, "Confession of Devotion: Is it Understood?" *Homiletic and Pastoral Review* 62 (1961) 235–238.

[17] Council of Trent, session XXII, chapter 2: "The holy Council teaches that this sacrifice is truly propitiatory (cf. canon 3). . . . Appeased by this sacrifice, the Lord grants the grace and gift of repentance and forgives crimes and sins however great" (DS 1743); see canon 3 (DS 1753). On the relationship between penance and the Eucharist, see the following: A. Bouley, "Eucharist: Our Reconciliation and Peace," *Catholic Charismatic* 1 (1976) 8–11; J. Dallen, "Eucharist and Penance," *Worship* 50 (1976) 324–328; J. G. Davies, "The Eucharist and the Remission of Sins," *Church Quarterly Review* 162 (1961) 50–58; J. G. Davies, *The Spirit, the Church, and the Sacraments,* London, 1954, 128ff.; E. J. Kilmartin, "Eucharist and Reconciliation," in "The Eucharist in Recent Literature," *Theological Studies* 32 (1971) 254–260; J. J. Quinn, "The Lord's Supper and Forgiveness of Sin," *Worship* 42 (1968) 281–291; A. Tegels, "Chronicle: The Eucharist and Reconciliation," *Worship* 42 (1968) 309–311; J.-M. Tillard, "The Bread and the Cup of Reconciliation," *Sacramental Reconciliation,* ed. E. Schillebeeckx, 38–54; J.-M. Tillard, "The Eucharist, *Pasch of God's People,* Staten Island, N.Y., 1967, 195–210.

[18] By way of complement to the present chapter, the reader may consult: C. McAuliffe, "Penance and Reconciliation with the Church," *Theological Studies* 26 (1965) 1–39; B. de Vaux Saint-Cyr, "Le Mystère de la réconciliation: Réconciliation avec Dieu, réconciliation avec l'Eglise," *Maison-Dieu,* no. 90 (1967) 132–154; C. F. Curran, "The Sacrament of Penance Today," *Worship* 43 (1969), 510–31, 590–619; 44 (1970) 2–19; F. J. Connell, "The Sacrament of Penance as Reconciliation with the Church," *American Ecclesiastical Review* 154 (1966) 134ff.; G. McCauley, "The Ecclesial Nature of the Sacrament of Penance," *Worship* 36 (1962) 212–222.

Notes to Chapter 6, pp. 77–80

[1] See F. Charrière, "Le pouvoir d'ordre et le pouvoir de juridiction dans le sacrement de pénitence," *Dictionnaire de théologie catholique* 23:191–213; L. Ott, *Fundamentals of Catholic Dogma*, tr. J. P. Lynch (St. Louis, 1954) 438; C. Journet, *The Church of the Word Incarnate* 1, tr. A. H. C. Downes (New York, 1955) 171–72.

[2] Since the powers of orders and jurisdiction are still important in the Church's practice, I refer readers to the diocesan *pagellae,* or lists of faculties, that indicate the canonical regulations that are still in force.

[3] In obeying this requirement, the rite will respond to one of the basic directives of the liturgical reform: "In sacred celebrations a more ample, more varied, and more suitable reading from sacred scripture should be restored" (*Constitution on the Sacred Liturgy,* no. 35; Flannery, 12).

[4] For the points of view that govern the new rite, note the Introduction to the Rite itself (nos. 1–40) as well as *Study Text 4., op. cit.;* R. Keifer and F. R. McManus, *The Rite of Penance: Commentaries, 1: Understanding the Document,* Washington, D.C., 1975; E. M. Jeep, ed., *The Rite of Penance: Commentaries, 2: Implementing the Rite,* Washington, D.C., 1976; N. Mitchell, ed. *The Rite of Penance: Commentaries, 3: Background and Directions,* Washington, D.C., 1978; F. Sottocornola, "A Look at the New Rite of Penance," Washington, D.C., USCC, 1975.

[5] *Rite of Penance,* no. 22.

[6] "Even if they acknowledge that the private portion of the rite and the individual absolution have a certain value, a number of priests are reluctant to hear the accusations and to give the absolution in a 'rather mechanical' fashion. The limitations of time seem to them to detract from the authenticity that had been attained in the first part of the communal celebration" (from the Canadian evaluation of communal penance rites done in 1974 by G. Bergeron, J-P. Duchesne, and C. Farley).

[7] *Rite of Penance,* no. 31.

[8] *Rite of Penance,* no. 35c.

[9] Here we have one of the reasons for not giving general absolution in connection with some other liturgical celebration already planned. Making the penance celebration entirely separate will prevent any ambiguity and will make clear the intention of those who desire to be reconciled with and in the Church.

[10] *De civitate Dei* XXI, 27, 5 (PL 41:750); see B. Häring, *The Law of Christ,* tr. E. G. Kaiser, 1 (Westminster, Md., 1961) 350–364.

[11] See above, chapter 3, note 5.

[12] It is difficult to understand and, above all, difficult to explain why the pastoral leader of a base community, who has received a mission, cannot also place the sacramental sign of reconciliation.

[13] *Rite of Penance,* nos. 38–40.

[14] For additional material on communal penance, consult such works as Bishops of Holland, "Public Celebration of Penance: A Pastoral Letter," *Worship* 40 (1966) 276–280; F. T. Hurley, "Communal Absolution: Anatomy of a Decision," *America* 127 (23 Sept 1972) 203–206; L. Orsy, "Communal Penance: Some Preliminary Questions on Sin and Sacrament," *Worship* 47 (1973) 338–345; C. Peter, "The New Forms for Communal Penance: Will They Help?" *Worship* 47 (1973) 2–10; K. Rahner, "Communal Penance Services and Individual Confession," *Theology Digest* 21 (1973)

139–142; P. Samway, "Faith and Communal Penance," *Worship* 43 (1969) 390–403; C. M. Whitley, "Understanding and Attitudes: Some Suggestions for Appreciating Communal Penance," *Review for Religious* 30 (1971) 218–227.

For further discussion of general absolution, see D. J. Dease, "General Confession and Absolution," *Worship* 51 (1977) 536–545; J. Gallen, "General Sacramental Absolution, Pastoral Remarks on Pastoral Norms," *Theological Studies* 34 (1973) 114–121; D. Krause, *et al., General Absolution: Toward a Deeper Understanding,* Chicago, Federation of Diocesan Liturgical Commissions, 1978; A. Tegels, "Chronicle: Instruction on General Absolution," *Worship* 46 (1972) 570–571 and 48 (1974) 550–553; M. Zalba, "Normae pastorales circa absolutionem sacramentalem generali modo impertiendam. Commentarium," *Notitiae* 8 (1972) 312–317 (text), 317–326 (commentary); comments in Bishops' Committee on the Liturgy (BCL) *Newsletter* 8/9–10 (1972), 11/4 (April 1975), 12 (Sept. 1976), 13 (March 1977).

On the subject of mortal and venial sin, see H. Allard, "New Views on Mortal Sin," *Clergy Review* 57 (1972) 468–471; M. Oraison et al., *Sin. Its Reality and Nature: An Historical Survey,* New York, 1962; P. DeLetter, "Sacramental Forgiveness of Venial Sin," *Ephemerides theologicae Lovanienses,* 30 (1954) 54–63; P. DeLetter, "Venial Sin: Paradox and Illogicality," *Irish Theological Quarterly* 22 (1955) 258–264.